DEMOCRATIC EFFICIENCY

**Inequality, Representation, and Public Policy Outputs
in the United States and Worldwide**

By

Lee Ryan Miller

authorHOUSE

1663 LIBERTY DRIVE, SUITE 200
BLOOMINGTON, INDIANA 47403
(800) 839-8640
www.authorhouse.com

First published by AuthorHouse 09/28/04

ISBN: 1-4184-0163-3 (e)
ISBN: 1-4184-0162-5 (sc)

Library of Congress Control Number: 2002095307

Printed in the United States of America
Bloomington, Indiana

This book is printed on acid-free paper.

Cover designed by George Chun-Han Wang.

To Ron Rogowski, for teaching me most of
what I know about the discipline of political science,
and to Shelley Berkley, for giving me a peek inside
the black box of politics.

CONTENTS

Preface

This is a book about the benefits and drawbacks of democracy. Part I begins with an exploration of democratic theory, and presents some evidence of the benefits of dispersing political power widely within a society. Part II focuses on the operation of the United States Congress.

This book is designed to be a supplemental text in a variety of political science courses. Part I is well-suited for an in-depth evaluation of democracy within the context of advanced courses in comparative politics, American politics, political theory, or other areas of the social sciences. Part II presents a detailed description of Congress appropriate for introductory American politics courses.

Acknowledgements

Part I of this book was inspired by the political science doctoral dissertation that I wrote at UCLA. I wish to thank the Center for International and Strategic Affairs (now the Center for International Relations) and the Pew Foundation for a fellowship that helped me to develop my dissertation proposal. I also wish to thank my committee members—Ronald Rogowski, James MacQueen, Richard Rosecrance, and Arthur Stein—for giving me valuable feedback. Thanks also to my late friends, Jim Rowe and Gary Trunk, for their editorial assistance. I miss them both greatly.

Part II came out of a week-long visit to Washington, DC. I wish to thank the School to Careers Program at the Community College of Southern Nevada for providing a grant in support of my research. I also wish to thank Congresswoman Shelley Berkley and her wonderful staff for welcoming me into their offices and their lives. I also extend my thanks to Mike Green, for his comments on earlier drafts.

Thanks also to Anita Chun for the countless hours she spent editing and proofreading this manuscript, and to George Chun-Han Wang for designing a beautiful cover.

Acknowledgements

Most importantly, I must thank my dear wife Beth for her patience and support throughout the many years and many incarnations of this project.

PART I

Inequality, Representation, and Comparative Policy Outputs

Part I of this book develops a model of the government policymaking process. This model takes into account the impact of the distribution of power in society on policy output. It focuses in particular on the impact of the distribution of economic resources and the impact of interest groups on the policymaking process, paying particular attention to inequality in the distribution of income and the power of organized labor.

Each chapter in Part I focuses on a different policy output. Each reviews the relevant scholarship in the disciplines of political science and economics and evaluates the model through statistical analysis.

In terms of classroom use, Part I is written at a level appropriate for advanced undergraduates and graduate students in the social sciences.

1

A Theory of Democratic Efficiency

What's So Great About Democracy?

Democracy is a system of government that seems to be coming back into style. Since the U.S.S.R. collapsed a decade ago, most of its former constituent republics and satellite states have taken steps toward establishing democratic political systems. Furthermore, large numbers of dictatorships in the Third World, which formerly were supported by either superpower, have also joined the democratization bandwagon. The question is: What's so great about democracy?

I offer no philosophical argument for democracy. That debate extends back to ancient Athens. Real-life politics have historically focused on practical concerns, and countless statesmen have dismissed the philosophical justifications for democratic rule, stating simply, "democracy is a luxury we can ill afford."

During the years preceding the end of the Cold War, scholars began to recognize two unusual characteristics of democratic countries: (1) they tend not to go to war against each other and (2) they tend to be the most economically successful states. Each of these observations is remarkable, and each has spawned a separate, burgeoning literature. Scholars such as Michael Doyle (1986), David Lake (1992), and Zeev Maoz and Bruce Russett (1993) have developed the literature on "democratic peace," the phenomenon that democracies rarely go to war with other democracies. Others, such as Douglas C. North (1981) and Mancur Olson (1993), have focused on how certain legal and political structures have made democracies the most economically successful countries in the world. Part I of this book will attempt to bridge the gap between these two literatures, to explain how democratic policymaking leads to *both* democratic peace and democratic economic superiority.

Michael Doyle was one of the first scholars to demonstrate that democracies have never gone to war against each other in modern times. It is a remarkable coincidence that, despite having fought two wars against each other, relations between the U.S. and Great Britain began to improve after the Americans abolished slavery and as the British began to expand suffrage in the latter part of the nineteenth century. It is equally remarkable that, after centuries of shifting alliances, all of the democratic states in Europe ended up on the same side in both world wars. Just as peculiar, despite centuries of rivalry and warfare, Western Europe has experienced an absence of warfare since democracy became the norm in the region after World War II.

Doyle claims that the common liberal ideology of democracies, as well as their common interests and institutional factors, are responsible for their unusual international behavior. He points out that democratic governments base their legitimacy on the contention that democracy is the only legitimate form of government. Democratic governments must depict their foreign enemies as "enemies of democracy" in order to mobilize political opinion in favor of war. Thus, they find it very difficult to go to war against other democracies, because a war with another democracy would undermine the legitimacy of democratic government.[1]

Doyle's analysis seems plausible initially. But he draws an arbitrary distinction between those states that he

---

[1] Maoz and Russett (1993) provide evidence that democracies are constrained from going to war against each other by institutional constraints on the ability of democratic leaders to go to war, as well norms of compromise and cooperation between democracies. Owen (1994) argues that institutional constraints permit the moral constraints to have an impact. Layne (1994) and Spiro (1994) disagree with the democratic peace thesis. Layne does four case studies of "near-misses" of war between democracies and concludes that reasons other than moral or institutional constraints had prevented war. Spiro compares all possible pairings of countries to the number of wars that actually occurred. Since war occurred infrequently in relation to the number of possible pairings, and since democracies represent a minority of countries, he concludes that random chance can explain the lack of war between democracies. This clever analysis, however, is flawed. With the exception of a few great powers having the ability to project force across oceans, it is much easier (and therefore, much more likely) for countries to go to war with neighboring countries than with countries thousands of miles away. Since democracies tend to be clustered together geographically (Western Europe, U.S./Canada, Australia/New Zealand, etc.) they should be more likely, *ceteris paribus*, to go to war against each other. If Spiro's study were to take this into account, I expect that his conclusions would lend support to the existence of a democratic peace.

defines as "liberal democracies" and those that supposedly do not fit this definition. In addition, he fails to explain why democracies tend to be more successful than non-democracies, as evidenced by the gradual historical trend toward greater democracy within individual states, the growing number of democracies worldwide, and the fact that most of the richest countries in the world are democracies.

David A. Lake (1992) further examines the phenomenon of democratic peace. He uses a formal model to illustrate that there are weaker expansionist tendencies among democracies than non-democracies. Lake also presents empirical evidence that democracies have been more successful in war than non-democracies. Since 1846 democracies have prevailed in 81% of the wars they have fought against non-democracies. Lake suggests three reasons for this: (1) democracies tend to form overwhelming counter-coalitions against expansionist autocracies, (2) democracies are better able to marshal their resources for a war effort than are autocracies, and (3) democratic government tends to create fewer economic distortions than non-democratic government and to make democracies wealthier than non-democracies.

Lake's first explanation is consistent with Doyle's theory of democratic peace. He argues that democracies tend not to fight against each other, but on the contrary, tend to form coalitions to resist expansionist non-democracies. The philosophical and institutional similarities of democracies make it very difficult for their governments to go to war against one another. This makes democracies natural allies. Such alliances not only make it easier for democracies to resist aggression by non-democracies, but it also means that they can devote fewer resources to defense in peacetime, since they do not have to fear attack by other democracies, and they can rely on the help of their democratic allies if they themselves are attacked.

Lake's second reason is that democracies are not only different from non-democracies, but institutionally superior. According to Lake, democratic governments enjoy greater public support for their policies, and therefore can rely upon the public to make a greater level of sacrifice in times of war. Thus, democratic governments "enjoy a greater extractive capacity for any given level of national wealth."[2] Although Lake does not present much empirical support for this claim, the work of several other scholars does support it. For example, despite the Nazis' totalitarian control over the German economy during World War II, the British were still able to devote a higher proportion of their GNP to defense.[3] In both world wars, the democracies were ultimately victorious, largely due to their superior ability to mobilize resources. Furthermore, democracies are better able than non-democracies to finance their war efforts because they find it easier to borrow money and, when they do, they pay lower interest rates.[4]

Lake's third reason for democratic superiority in war is that democratic government creates fewer economic distortions than non-democratic government, allowing democratic countries to become wealthy; this allows democracies to accumulate financial and economic resources to draw upon, should war become necessary.

---

[2] Lake (1992), p. 30.
[3] United States (1945); Klein (1959).
[4] Schultz and Weingast (1994). Although his analysis does not differentiate countries by level of democracy, Tilly (1990) makes a similar point with regard to the Dutch Republic, the Republic of Venice, and Great Britain.

With the exception of semi-democratic Singapore and a handful of countries with tiny populations and vast amounts of oil, the fifty countries with the highest income per capita in the world[5] are all democracies.[6] Moreover, of the hundred countries with the highest income per capita,[7] eighty-three are indisputably democracies. In fact, hardly any countries with at least a decade of uninterrupted democratic rule are poor. In contrast, of the hundred countries with the lowest income per capita,[8] at most sixteen could be described as democracies.

Mancur Olson (1993) argues that democracies are more economically successful than non-democracies because the former provide a more fertile environment for private investment. Olson contends that countries with a history of democratic government do this by guaranteeing the protection of property rights[9] and the enforcement of contracts in perpetuity; under non-democratic regimes, such guarantees

---

[5] Income per capita figures for the top fifty countries range from $10,050 to $42,060. See World Bank (2002).

[6] For determining whether or not a country was a democracy, I relied on Freedom House (2002). The oil-rich non-democracies that made the list of the fifty richest countries were Brunei, Kuwait, and the United Arab Emirates. The list also included entries that were not really countries at all, but instead territories with only limited autonomy—Macao and Hong Kong (China), and New Caledonia (France).

[7] Income per capita figures for the top hundred countries range from $2,080 to $42,060. See World Bank (2002).

[8] Income per capita figures for each of the bottom hundred countries was $1,820 or less. See World Bank (2002).

[9] Olson's work on this subject builds upon the foundation constructed by North (1981). North chronicles the historical development of the institutions embodying property rights, which he claims have been responsible for economic growth and development.

are threatened by the whims of those in power, or (when the leaders have a good track record) uncertainty about the whims of their successors. Olson shows that democratic institutions can limit the rent-seeking behavior of those in power.

This institutional superiority of democracy has only increased with economic development. Modern industry is becoming increasingly knowledge-intensive; sovereignty[10] is organized in democratic states in a fashion uniquely suited to an economy that relies heavily upon human capital in the production of wealth.[11]

One can draw an analogy to the firm. An information-intensive enterprise, like a computer software company, tends to raise capital through the sale of stock, whereas an enterprise more dependent on tangible assets, such as a trucking firm, tends to be privately owned and to raise capital through borrowing. Why is this? If the firm goes bankrupt, investors in the trucking firm can seize the firm's income-generating assets (the trucks), whereas investors in the software firm cannot seize the knowledge of the software designers. Therefore, those who invest in the software company have good reason to insist upon voting control.[12]

---

[10] By sovereignty, I mean the power to make laws governing the society and/or economy.

[11] Robert J. Barro (1991) demonstrates that the growth rate of real per capita GDP is positively related to the level of human capital in a given country.

[12] Similarly, Williamson (1985) notes that when a firm's assets cannot easily be seized by a lender, the lender usually requires equity as collateral (p. 307).

Economists have found that the more dependent on human capital is a firm's production, the more likely is that firm to employ profit-sharing schemes as a way to motivate its workers (or, in economic terms, to employ its human capital more efficiently).[13] Such schemes imply a recognition of the power of workers in determining productivity and profits. One extreme example of this is the practice, common among high technology companies, for the firm to give its employees equity as a benefit of employment. Since slavery is illegal, the firm cannot own its productive (human) capital. The owners of this capital (the workers themselves), once again, demand voting control.[14]

John Jay, one of the authors of the *Federalist Papers* and a founder of American democracy, once said, "The people who own the country ought to govern it." Democracy is the political system that makes this possible. Just as in the case of the software company, the more knowledge-intensive is the nation's economy, the more likely are those who have a stake in the economy to demand voting rights. Thus,

---

[13] Alchian & Demsetz (1972).

[14] Klein, Alchian, and Crawford (1978) illustrate this with their discussion of "appropriable quasi-rents." When a firm rents its productive capital, the owner of that capital may have the ability to extract "quasi-rents" from the firm. For example, a newspaper publisher tends to own—rather than rent—its printing press. This is because, if the publisher were to rent the press, the owner of the press could demand an increase in the rent, knowing that the publisher would pay a high price (such as not publishing anything for a few days) if s/he tried to find another printing press. In the case of human-capital-intensive production, the cost of finding and training replacement workers can be costly. The firm therefore avoids the problem of appropriable quasi-rents—not by buying its productive (human) capital (which is illegal), but instead by allowing the human capital to own the firm.

the more technologically advanced is a state, the more likely it is to be a democracy. Given that the most technologically advanced states tend to have the highest per capita incomes, one should also expect the richest states to be democracies.

According to Samuel P. Huntington, "a highly developed, industrialized economy and the complex economy that it implies cannot be governed efficiently by authoritarian means. Decision-making is necessarily dispersed, and hence power is shared and rule must be based on consent."[15] The organizational advantage of democracy over other forms of political organization is magnified as production in a country's economy becomes increasingly knowledge-intensive. The more knowledge-intensive is the economy, the more vital quick and efficient communications become. Democratic institutions provide the most hospitable environment possible for unfettered communication.[16] For this I can offer a simple illustration. Try to imagine a totalitarian state in which most people have access to electronic communications like fax machines, photocopiers, and the Internet. It could not exist, because a government can effectively suppress dissent only by suppressing communication. Otherwise, it would find the sheer volume of information too large to monitor. Now try to imagine a present-day advanced economy in which most citizens have no access to electronic communications. It also cannot exist. Today's most advanced economies require the quick and efficient dissemination of information.

---

[15] Huntington (1984), p. 413.

[16] David E. Apter (1955 and 1973), while studying political development in post-colonial Ghana, was one of the first scholars to recognize the inverse relationship between information and coercion.

Defining Democracy

Before I further develop my argument regarding the benefits of democracy, I need to define the term "democracy." This is no easy task. Contradictory definitions abound. The word comes from the Greek "demos," meaning "people" and "-kratia," meaning government—in other words, government by the people. But this term was meant to distinguish this political arrangement from the monarchies, tyrannies, and oligarchies of the day. Ancient Athens was the first country to call its political institutions by this name. There, political officials were chosen by lot and most political decisions were debated and voted upon by the citizenry as a whole.[17] On the other hand, women and slaves were barred from the political process.

The Webster's Ninth New Collegiate Dictionary[18] defines democracy as follows:

> 1a : government by the people; *esp*: rule of the majority b: a government in which the supreme power is vested in the people and exercised by them directly or indirectly through a system of representation usu. involving periodically held free elections 2: a political unit that has a democratic government ... 4: the common people esp. when constituting the source of political authority 5: the absence of hereditary or arbitrary class distinctions or privileges

This is certainly a broad definition that could encompass diverse political systems. Indeed, throughout history, people have called a variety of political systems by the name "democracy." In the words of Karl de Schweinitz, Jr.:

---

[17] See Aristotle (1974), pp. 69 – 200.
[18] *Webster's* (1985), p. 338.

> Democracy is one of those troublesome words which means all things to all people. Like motherhood and patriotism, it is thought to be a noble condition and so is evoked by politicians, publicists, preachers, and demagogues to prove their unsullied intentions and just claim to popular support.[19]

In the Cold War era, the meaning of the term "democracy" became an intense ideological conflict. The Communist states claimed to be true democracies because, in their societies, power was not allocated on the basis of birth or wealth. On the other hand, the average citizen in Communist countries such as the German *Democratic* Republic, could not debate any important political issues, and had no choice when it came to voting.

The Western "democracies" have tended to emphasize institutional—rather than social—factors as the determinants of democracy. Many Western political scientists have exhibited this same tendency in their definitions of democracy. Schumpeter defines democracy as an "institutional arrangement for arriving at political decisions in which individuals acquire the power to decide by means of a competitive struggle for the people's vote."[20] Similarly, Lipset defines democracy as

> a political system which supplies regular constitutional opportunities for changing the governing officials, and a social mechanism which permits the largest possible part of the population to influence major decisions by choosing among contenders for political office.[21]

---

[19] De Schweinitz (1964), p.12.

[20] Schumpeter (1942), p. 269.

[21] Lipset (1960), p.45.

Such scholars have defined rather vaguely as "democracy" political systems which afford citizens the opportunity on a regular basis to elect representatives who will wield the power to make laws. There are some countries, such as Mexico prior to 2000, which have democratic institutions and which hold regular, free, multi-party elections, but in which electoral fraud keeps the same party perpetually in power. In other countries, (such as Colombia and southern Italy, for example) there are democratically-elected governments, but those governments do not really control the country.

One possible solution to the problem of defining democracy is to approach it as a matter of degree: Is Country X more or less democratic than Country Y?[22] One might argue, for example, that political systems with the above characteristics are less democratic than those found in the countries of northwestern Europe, the U.S., Canada, etc. The political institutions found in the latter group, however, are quite diverse. Is a country with a powerful president, such as the United States and France, more democratic than one where the executive power lies in the hands of a cabinet, as in Sweden or Belgium? Is a country with a bicameral legislature more democratic than a country with a unicameral legislature? Is it more democratic to hold elections every two years than to hold them every five years? Does the ratio of citizens to representatives imply anything about how democratic a country is? Are single-member districts or multi-member districts more democratic?

---

[22] For a good review of various techniques used to measure democracy, see Bollen (1980).

The answers to these questions are far from clear. The answer that one chooses to give reveals more about the analyst's personal preferences and cultural biases than about the nature of democracy. If I define presidential systems as more democratic than parliamentary systems, for instance, my definition may merely be a reflection of the fact that I have lived all my life in a country with a presidential system. There is no objective way to justify such a choice. But ignoring these differences eliminates all possible points of comparison between countries. If one focuses solely on the institutions themselves, the very diversity of democratic political institutions seems to render it impossible to measure democracy in a culturally-unbiased fashion.

Other scholars look not at the institutions *per se*, but at the effects of the political system on personal and/or economic freedom. For example, Kenneth Bollen (1980) creates a scale of political democracy based on the following factors: (1) the degree of press freedom, (2) the degree to which organized opposition is allowed, (3) the degree to which the government attempts to curtail political activity, (4) the degree to which elections are free from corruption and coercion, (5) whether the members of the executive and legislature are elected, and (6) whether the legislature has effective power in determining government policies. Many other scholars have constructed similar indices of democracy.[23] The trouble with them all, from the standpoint of doing empirical research, is that they are composed of subjective ratings on some particular set of criteria. What I seek is a definition of democracy that will encompass all of these in-

---

[23] See, for example, Arat (1988), Coleman (1960), Coulter (1975), Freedom House (2002), and Jackman (1973).

stitutional differences while permitting me to objectively compare the degree of democracy cross-nationally.

Robert A. Dahl (1971) provides a definition of democracy that makes this possible. According to his definition, government policy is formulated based solely upon the preferences of all citizens, and the preferences of all citizens are weighted equally in the policymaking process.[24]

In order for this to occur, citizens must have unconstrained opportunities to do the following:

1. To formulate their preferences
2. To signify their preferences to their fellow citizens and the government by individual and collective action
3. To have their preferences weighted equally in the conduct of the government, that is, weighted with no discrimination because of the content or source of the preferences[25]

Part I of this book will focus on the third criterion. It is not my intention to minimize the importance of the other two criteria. I believe that access to education and a free press providing a variety of viewpoints (#1) are essential to the healthy maintenance of democracy. Similarly, I believe that freedom of expression and association, the right to vote, etc. (#2) are vital components of democracy. I focus on the third criterion for two reasons. First of all, most research to date, as indicated by the works that I previously cited, focus exclusively on the first and second criteria. Secondly, I believe that the third criterion is the most important of the three, primarily because the other two are to a large extent dependent upon it.

---

[24] Dahl (1971), pp. 1–2.
[25] Dahl (1971), p. 2.

The third criterion is the distribution of political power in society. The more political power a person has, by definition, the greater weight the government places on that person's preferences. The more equally power is distributed in the country, the more equally the government will weigh the preferences of citizens.

The distribution of power has a profound effect upon Dahl's other two criteria. Education may be necessary for an informed electorate. But a government chooses whether or not to allow elections, however informed the electorate is. On the other hand, to the extent that people wish to have educational opportunities, if the government heeds their policy preferences, it will spend the money necessary to provide those opportunities. After all, virtually all educational institutions throughout the world are funded at least in part by governments.

Similarly, a free press plays a vital role in educating citizens about important political issues, but a free press cannot force a government to listen to the preferences of its citizens. A government can easily censor the press, if it does not like what is written about it (and, sadly, most governments in the world do just this). On the other hand, to the extent that people wish to be well-informed, if the government heeds their policy preferences, it will minimize its restrictions on press freedom.

The same can be said about freedom of association, expression, and the right to vote. The existence of such rights and freedoms alone cannot force a government to heed the preferences of its citizenry. Governments can (and frequently do) restrict such rights and freedoms. To the extent that people value their freedom, and to the extent that the government heeds their preferences, the government will minimize restrictions on their rights and freedoms.

I do not claim that the third criterion captures all of the information contained in the other two criteria. But I do claim that it captures a good deal. Therefore, for the sake of analytical simplicity, I will focus exclusively upon the third criterion, the distribution of power within society. Henceforth, within the context of this chapter, I define democracy as follows: Democracy is the equality with which political power is distributed within a given country. In other words, the more equally power is distributed within Country X, the more democratic is Country X.[26]

What I mean by political power is the power to influence the lawmaking process of the government. Why would one want to do this? Because public policy can have an enormous impact on private interests.

For example, there are several ways that the government can help or harm the interests of a given firm. The most direct way is for the government to provide a subsidy. Agriculture is one of the more notorious subsidy recipients, but there are many others. Secondly, the government can buy goods from the firm. The U.S. government spends billions of dollars each year purchasing goods ranging from pencils to aircraft carriers. Thirdly, tariff and trade policy can have an enormous impact on profits/losses. Scarcely a day goes by without some industry requesting increased protection from foreign imports. Finally, government regulation can act to protect the profits of firms in a given industry or can add significantly to the costs of firms. Regulation of air travel fares

---

[26] I will explain how to measure the distribution of political power later in this chapter.

used to protect the profits of U.S. airlines. In 1994, lobbying by a number of industries defeated a proposal that would have required all firms in the United States to provide health insurance for their employees.

Anything that affects the interests of firms affects the interests of individuals. Many citizens are stockholders; the value of their assets rises and falls with profits and losses. Even more citizens receive the majority of their income in the form of salaries and wages. When business is bad, firms tend to defer salary increases and to lay off workers. Finally, virtually all citizens are consumers. We all feel the impact of tariffs, subsidies, regulations, etc. in the form of changes in prices. The government has the power to profoundly affect private interests—a fact that is vividly illustrated by the legions of lobbyists who besiege the state and federal governments in the United States.

A Model of Government Decision-Making

Now it is time to create a model to illustrate the connection between the distribution of power in a society (the degree of democracy) and the policies adopted by its government. Like all models, mine simplifies reality in order to focus on a few key ideas. The model that I propose defines government as the mechanism by which the preferences of citizens are translated into policy:

CITIZENS' PREFERENCES
(weighted according to political power)
↓
GOVERNMENT
↓
POLICY

This model can describe the operations of democratic and non-democratic governments alike. All governments, by definition, give greater weight to the preferences of those citizens with more political power than to the preferences of those with less political power. Thus, the governments of those societies with a more equal distribution of power (the more democratic societies, by my definition) should adopt policies which better reflect the preferences of their citizens than societies with a less equal distribution of power (less democratic countries). To the extent that citizens—rather than some paternalistic elite—know what is best for them (which is, after all, the fundamental principle of democracy), the policies of democratic governments should come closer to maximizing aggregate social welfare than the policies of non-democratic governments. In other words, democratic governments should adopt policies that benefit a larger percentage of their citizens than should the policies of non-democratic governments.

Essentially, democratic governments come closer than non-democratic governments to emulating the behavior of a benevolent social planner; that is, they do better at maximizing aggregate social welfare. Why is this the case? I suggest that democratic governments tend to be more efficient at translating social preferences into policy than non-democratic governments. They are more efficient because democratic institutions are structured to assimilate massive amounts of information (preferences) and translate that information into policy. Non-democratic governments, on the other hand, systematically exclude a large percentage of the information available (preferences) and follow policies that are either uninformed or benefit the policymakers at the expense of the rest of society.

Gary Becker (1983 & 1985) presents one powerful example of the greater efficiency of democratic policymaking. He shows that competition among interest groups yields more efficient taxation policies. The reason is that limiting the deadweight costs of tax collection is in the interest both of groups favoring and groups opposing increases in the size of government. Efficient taxation benefits the net recipients of government subsidies, because any deadweight costs that are eliminated are available for increases in such subsidies. By the same token, efficient taxation benefits the net contributors to government subsidies, because the deadweight costs (as well as the subsidies) come out of their pockets. Lower deadweight costs can yield higher government spending, tax cuts, or both. As long as government is responsive to pressures from their citizenry, such pressure should result in more efficient policies. But if the recipients of government subsidies know that the net contributors to those subsidies have no influence with the government, the subsidy recipients have little incentive to lobby for more efficient taxation policies. Thus, more open policymaking systems should be expected to devise more efficient ways of raising revenues, while less open systems should have little incentive for such innovation.[27]

Essentially, the more democratic the country, the more people the government has to please; the less democratic the country, the more people the government can ignore. The question is: how do democratic governments manage to digest the preferences of tens of millions of citizens? To answer this question, it would be helpful to look briefly at some basic microeconomics.

The collapse of Communism in Eastern Europe resolved one of the great conflicts in economic theory. It showed decisively that capitalism, as an economic system, was far superior to Communism. In more concrete terms, it revealed that the market is superior to central planning in the allocation of resources in a modern economy.[28]

Neoclassical economists have been arguing this for some time, and their influence in American society has been so great that few people stop to ponder *why* the market is more efficient. The answer is that the modern economy is so com-

---

[27] Machiavelli (1965) also argues that democratic government is more efficient and cost-effective. He argues that a "republican" (democratic) form of government would be more efficient for Florence than a princedom because the latter would require large expenditures on repression and coercion to remain in power.

[28] Economists, of course, have known this for a long time. The First Theorem of Welfare Economics states that "all market equilibria are Pareto efficient." The Second Theorem of Welfare Economics states, "if all agents have convex preference, then there will always be a set of prices such that each Pareto optimal allocation is a market equilibrium for an appropriate assignment of endowments." These theorems appear in most microeconomics textbooks. See, for example, Varian (1990), pp. 490–499.

plex that no central institution can collect, process, and act upon all information regarding supply and demand with the speed necessary to make central planning work. There is just too much information. But an individual actor (a consumer or a firm) in even the most complex economy does not need to know everything about supply and demand in all sectors of the economy in order to make a decision. S/he need only make calculations based on individual costs and benefits, which permits quick and decisive action. The aggregation of all of these small decisions makes up a system characterized by rapid adjustments to the allocation of resources, ensuring the most efficient allocation possible in the economy. This is how capitalism works.[29]

There are many real-life examples of how the greater dispersion of decision-making power creates greater efficiency. One is the organizational superiority of M-form (multi-divisional) corporations over U-form (unitary) corporations.[30] When a corporation reaches a certain size, it becomes impossible for a central management group to make all the decisions regarding the allocation of resources within that company. No one group of people can know everything necessary about the many varied activities of a very large company, or can process that information quickly enough to make decisions before market changes render those decisions out of date. Therefore, very large corporations tend not to be organized in a strictly hierarchical fashion, but in-

---

[29] Wittman (1989) attacks the assumption that market failure is more likely in democratic politics than in capitalist economics. He uses microeconomic analysis to demonstrate that democratic political markets operate as efficiently as do economic markets.

[30] See Williamson (1985), chapter 11.

stead are divided into a number of semi-independent divisions. The top management of such corporations, rather than managing all the activities of the corporation, instead act as coordinators between the divisions, intervening only in matters that affect the corporation as a whole. In other words, decisions are made at the lowest possible level.

Computer architecture provides an additional example of the superiority of decentralized decision-making power. Computers, like central planners and corporate managers, need to collect ("retrieve") and analyze ("process") massive amounts of information ("data"). Depending upon the amount of data and the intricacy of the operations that the computer must perform, this may take a long time. The traditional computer design is for a single central processing unit to retrieve the data from memory, to perform sequentially the operations necessary for processing those data, and to return the processed data to memory. The reason that this can take a long time is that data processing is done in a centralized fashion, as in a centrally-planned economy or a U-form corporation. Since the central processing unit can only do one task at a time, each operation necessary for processing the data must await the completion of the previous operation. Computer designers have partially overcome this drawback by designing ever-smaller circuitry. The smaller the circuitry, the shorter the distance that the electronic signals must travel in the computer, and thus, the faster the processing. Computer designers, however, have nearly reached the limits of efficiency improvement through miniaturization: circuits cannot be smaller than a single molecule. Therefore, many computer designers have been experimenting with ways to decentralize data processing as a way to improve efficiency. This approach is embodied in the twin concepts of distributed and parallel processing.[31]

Distributed processing occurs when processing is distributed among several processing units, while parallel processing occurs when various processing tasks are performed simultaneously. Such systems increase the speed (efficiency) at which data processing is performed. Rather than having to wait for a central planner (central processing unit) to slowly make decisions (perform data processing operations), decisions are made simultaneously in a decentralized fashion. Distributed and parallel systems promise great increases in data processing speed and efficiency.

These concepts have been put to good use by researchers seeking a cure for anthrax. Researchers at Oxford University had the herculean task of evaluating billions of candidate molecules.[32] 1.4 million people from 215 countries worldwide volunteered to assist them in their work. The volunteers downloaded a screensaver that analyzed bundles of 100 molecules at a time and sent the results back to the researchers via the Internet. In just twenty-four days, computers worldwide devoted 90,000 years of CPU time to the problem, narrowing the field of potential cures from 3.5 billion molecules to just 15,000 promising candidates.

Democracy possesses the same type of efficiency advantage as capitalism, M-form corporations, and distributed

---

[31] The implications of parallel processing for political systems are discussed by Gore (1992), pp. 358–359. There are countless books on distributed and parallel processing, most of which are highly technical. Crichlow (1988) and Sharp (1987) are among the most accessible to non-computer scientists.

[32] See National Public Radio (2002).

and parallel processing systems.[33] It allows decisions to be made at the lowest possible level. In a democracy, people process political information and weigh the costs and benefits, articulating their choices and preferences (in the same way that individual consumers affect aggregate demand) through voting and exercising their freedom of expression. In non-democratic systems, on the other hand, governments have difficulty collecting the information about the needs of their societies and, as a result, tend to make sub-optimal decisions. They also run into sticky collective action problems, because the cartels monopolizing political power have strong incentives to use that power to redirect economic resources toward themselves, rather than allowing the market to allocate resources such that they maximize the welfare of the society as a whole.[34] In other words, dictators and oligarchs should be expected to become wealthy from their positions, because they have the power to extract bribes and subsidies (political monopoly rents) for themselves and their individual economic interests. This diversion of economic resources from more productive uses, in general, retards economic growth.

Democracy should act as a check on such impulses by governments, because the electorate should be expected

---

[33] The more decentralized is its decision-making structure, in general, the better a given state should fare economically. This holds true even for democracies. Decision-making institutions that are too centralized may help to explain the ongoing economic problems faced by countries such as present-day Britain and France. For a discussion of the virtues of political decentralization from the standpoint of economic theory, see Tiebout (1956).

[34] Many of these ideas stem from the concepts developed by Olson (1982).

to demand policies benefiting themselves (the voters), *not* the people they elect to positions of power. Even when democratic officials become corrupt, democracy still limits their rent-seeking behavior. Dictators are able to demand a bribe nearly as valuable as the windfall to be captured by those who gain special favors in return for that bribe. Dictators like Ferdinand Marcos of the Philippines and Mobutu Sese Seko of Zaire accumulated enormous wealth in this way. But corrupt democratic officials accept remarkably "cheap bribes" that are substantially less than the windfall received by those who bribe them.[35] Corruption is costly to any society. But democracy limits the cost of corruption. In microeconomic terms, democratic societies lose only the cost of the bribe, while non-democratic societies can see the entire consumer surplus from a particular transaction transferred to a Swiss bank account. Democracy limits economically unproductive, rent-seeking behavior by political officials.

Democracy is thus efficient in two senses. First, democratic governments are more efficient than non-democratic governments at translating the preferences of their citizens into policies that reflect those preferences. Secondly, democratic governments tend to be better than non-democratic governments at adopting policies which promote the best interest of the largest number of people in society.

---

[35] Rasmusen and Ramseyer (1994). They survey the literature indicating that democratic legislators accept cheap bribes. They explain this phenomenon with a game theoretical model. It takes into account the electoral cost to *all* legislators (even those who vote against it) when a law passes which puts private above public interest, and also takes into account the coordination problem for corrupt legislators in an open society.

The more democratic a society, the more the policies of its government should maximize aggregate social welfare. The more influence the average citizen has on his/her government, the more beneficial should be the policies of that government to the interests of its average citizen.[36] Or, at least, this is what my model predicts if we assume that all governments are equally efficient at processing information. Policy output will not always be superior with greater input from the citizenry, any more than you can double the output of an automobile plant just by doubling the amount of steel delivered to it. You may face diminishing marginal returns because the plant machinery may be just too outmoded to handle the increase in inputs. Similarly, there are a number of institutional factors that can influence the efficiency of

---

[36] Of course, this assumes that citizens have access to the information necessary to make informed choices and that they feel sufficiently motivated to make their preferences known. These, I believe, are reasonable assumptions. To the extent that citizens can influence their governments, their most important interest should be to maintain that influence, or else they will have no way to protect their interests in the future. This implies that it is in citizens' interest to prevent their government from restricting their access to the information necessary to formulate their preferences. How much information an individual citizen chooses to consult is a decision which should be based on the marginal value of additional information in a particular subject area. But allowing the government to restrict access to such information limits the ability of citizens to look out for all of their interests, and thus is irrational. One should therefore expect great opposition to significant increases in the amount of censorship to which a society is subject. Similarly, although not all citizens will devote equal time and effort to conveying their preferences to the government, each citizen should be motivated to do so when s/he feels that a particular issue is important enough to warrant the effort.

the decision-making process, thereby affecting the marginal value of citizen input.

It is possible to have an equal distribution of power but have the government structured such that it is unable to reach a decision on certain questions. Some may argue that government is just a needless hindrance to the economy, but this viewpoint is simplistic and incorrect. Government action can be crucial for the operation of the economy. Although much maligned as strangling business with cumbersome regulations, business could not exist without the legal system enforced by the government. Furthermore, as Douglas North chronicles, government innovation in the field of property rights has fueled economic growth and progress through the ages, while lack of innovation has resulted in backwardness and economic stagnation.[37]

A government certainly has the power to harm the economy. But the economy cannot function without the government. It is impossible to buy or sell anything without a recognized system of property rights. Furthermore, such property rights are meaningless unless there exists some authority to enforce them. Otherwise, financial transactions tend to be made at gunpoint and the marketplace descends into anarchy.

In addition to defining and enforcing property rights, the government engages in countless other actions which reduce transaction costs, thereby facilitating commerce. Trade is usually uncertain and infrequent without a reliable transportation network, which often is constructed by—and usually regulated by—the government. But roads, railways, and airplane routes alone do not ensure widespread trade.

---

[37] North (1981).

Without rules governing their use, transportation networks would be fraught with collisions and other accidents, discouraging trade by causing unnecessary delays and by destroying merchandise. In addition, trade cannot occur without willing buyers. Governments do much to encourage consumerism by enforcing regulations to protect the health and safety of consumers.[38] Without such protections, fear would deter many consumers from making purchases. Such regulations also encourage commerce. The government must enforce property rights for the economy to exist at all, while government regulations can help to speed economic growth by reducing transaction costs. If government paralysis prevents innovations that would benefit the economy, then such government is inefficient, however democratic it is.

---

[38] It is true that the private sector can perform a similar function by providing consumers with information about which products to avoid. Publications such as *Consumer Reports* play this role. But the private sector often fails to provide accurate information. For example, *Consumer Reports* (1993) notes that the companies that rate the financial strength of insurance companies often enjoy a cozy relationship with the insurance companies that they rate. (Insurance companies usually pay them for rating them.) In most cases of insurance company collapse, the companies in question had received good ratings. Similar problems exist with regard to private sector entities providing information to investors. The Enron collapse revealed that auditors such as Arthur Anderson can turn a blind eye to shady accounting practices when the auditor also has lucrative consulting deals with the firms that they are auditing. Similarly, a New York state investigation and subsequent lawsuit against Merrill Lynch revealed that Wall Street analysts often advise investors to buy stocks that are poor risks when the analysts' firm does lucrative underwriting business with the firm whose stock they are evaluating. Although the private sector can provide information to help consumers make informed choices, in many cases, government regulation is a necessary correction for market failures related to asymmetric information.

The most efficient political system is one which has not only the most equal distribution of political power in the society, but also a central government quickly able to collect and to process the information necessary for decisive decisions in those areas where a central decision is necessary. I shall call this concept "democratic efficiency." A country's democratic efficiency (F) is a function of its degree of democracy (the distribution of power in society), or (D) and its government's decision-making efficiency (E). The partial derivative of each independent variable is positive. To the extent that one can measure the two components making up democratic efficiency, one should be able to explain the behavior of governments, including their international behavior.

$$F=F(D,E); \ \partial F/\partial D>0, \ \partial F/\partial E>0$$

Distribution of Wealth

How might one measure the distribution of political power? There are several options. One is the distribution of wealth. In a capitalist society, wealth provides access to political power. A wealthy person can directly affect the selection of political leadership, through such means as financing political campaigns, or in the case of non-democratic systems, financing coercive groups that install and maintain leaders in power. A poor person lacks such resources, and thus does not have as much influence.

The wealthy can also indirectly influence government policy. The owners of capital have great influence over a country's economy. They influence economic growth rates by deciding whether and where to invest their wealth.

Similarly, they affect unemployment levels when they decide to hire and lay off large numbers of employees. Such power influences the government to pursue policies that benefit the return on their investments. Otherwise, the owners of wealth will "lose confidence" in the government's policies, send their money overseas, and curtail hiring. This will result in an economic downturn, undermining support for the government.[39] Poor people, of course, lack such power. Thus, a more equal distribution of wealth should indicate a more equal distribution of political power.

Along these lines, the power of the labor movement could be a second indicator of the distribution of power in society. Indeed, as I shall soon demonstrate, the size of interest groups is related to the second component of democratic efficiency: the efficiency by which a government transforms social preferences into public policy.

Interest Groups

But first I should explain how interest groups fit into the policymaking process. In a political system where all citizens debate and vote on all questions of public policy, interest groups would likely play a limited role in policymaking. In most countries today, however, there are just too

---

[39] Przeworski and Wallerstein (1988) critique the idea of "structural dependence of the state on capital" by showing that governments can impose tax rates as high as they wish without creating incentives for capitalists to curtail investment, as long as investments are not subject to taxation. One must note, however, that few, if any, governments obtain all of their revenue from taxes on consumption. Furthermore, there are other issues besides taxation which affect the return on investments, such as anti-trust, worker safety, consumer protection, and environmental regulations.

many citizens for such a system of direct democracy to be workable. Consequently, today's so-called "democratic" states are governed by elected representatives. In these societies, power is not equally distributed. This creates a great incentive for citizens to pool their resources with other citizens having similar interests, and as a group to pressure their government. If all groups were equally powerful, this would not greatly affect the distribution of power in society. In fact, some groups are more powerful than others, and the more powerful groups, just like dictators and oligarchs, tend to divert economic resources to themselves, away from more productive uses. The society as a whole loses out.[40]

It is unrealistic to assume that any democratic government could prevent people from forming interest groups.[41] At best, the optimistic supporter of democracy can hope that "special interest groups" will become so encompassing as to lose the "special." The larger a group is, the closer its interests coincide with those of society as a whole. Thus, in a democratic society, the more inclusive are the interest groups, the more equal will be the distribution of political power, and the more efficient (in the sense of providing for the needs of the society) will be the government that those groups are trying to influence. This is another possible measure of the first component of democratic efficiency.

Peak associations, or large interest groups representing key sectors in the economy, are not inconsistent with the decentralization of power that is central to the concept of democratic

---

[40] See Olson (1982).

[41] Nor would that necessarily be desirable, as a society of uncooperative, atomized individuals would not likely be the stuff of which healthy democracies are made.

efficiency. I shall present two justifications for favoring peak associations over special interest groups, the first economic, the second organizational.

A few large interest groups can have a benign or even positive effect upon the process of legislation, while large numbers of small special interest groups create negative distortions in the legislative process and major misallocations of resources in the economy. This contrast is due to the effect of organizational size upon rent-seeking behavior. All interest groups attempt to influence legislation and government policies to the benefit of their members. In such attempts, however, small size provides a notable advantage. This is because the benefit per member of a small group receiving a government subsidy, tax break, etc. easily exceeds the cost per member of society. The members of the group therefore have a great incentive to lobby hard for the subsidy, while no one has any great incentive to oppose them. While the cost of the rent-seeking behavior of a single special interest group may be minimal, the cumulative cost of the behavior of many such groups can be enormous.

A few large groups are preferable in this regard. But as the membership of an interest group increases, the benefit per group member declines, while the cost per member of society increases. Given that members of the interest group are also members of society, they receive a share of both the cost and the benefit of the subsidy. If the group is large enough, its interests become similar to those of society as a whole, and there is no incentive for rent-seeking behavior. For large groups, subsidies are no more than taking a dollar out of the left pocket and placing it in the right.[42]

---

[42] See Olson (1982).

Gary Becker (1983 & 1985) makes two points which imply that large groups are preferable to small ones. The smaller and more numerous interest groups are, the more "cross-hauling" occurs. "Cross-hauling" in this sense[43] occurs when members of the same group both receive subsidies and pay for the subsidies of other groups through taxation. Given that redistribution incurs administrative deadweight costs, it is clearly more efficient to transfer money directly from Peter to Paul, rather than each transferring money to the other (with the net balance going to Paul). The larger the interest groups are, the less group memberships overlap, and the less "cross-hauling" occurs.

Becker's second point is that lobbying itself involves deadweight costs. Resources spent on lobbying could be invested in something that produces economic growth, rather than mere redistribution of the returns from the productive investments of others. Furthermore, lobbying activities by opposing groups tend to cancel each other out. To the extent that spending more money on lobbying increases the chances that legislation will benefit a given group, interest groups should be expected to be spending increasing amounts on lobbying just to make sure that opposing groups do not gain the upper hand. In the U.S., the spiraling cost of political campaigns (which are funded primarily by interest groups) provides an indication of this. If opposing groups were able to surmount this prisoner's dilemma and were to limit the amount that they spend on lobbying, they would save money (lower deadweight costs) without any lessening of their political

---

[43] "Cross-hauling" normally refers to a practice in freight-hauling.

influence. Organized consultation between government policymakers and leaders of peak associations lessens the need for expenditure on lobbying, thereby minimizing deadweight costs.

Not only do large interest groups help a country to avoid the pitfalls of rent-seeking behavior, but they also make the legislative process more efficient. This is despite the centralization that comes with large size. The reason for this is that peak associations focus on the common functional set of interests held by members. For example, workers have a common set of interests distinct from that of corporate management.[44]

In fact, despite their large membership, peak associations are probably better organized to represent people's interests than individuals representing small, geographically-based districts in a legislature, which is the norm in English-speaking countries. For whereas the leaders of

---

[44] I am not arguing that all individuals in the same group have precisely the same interests, but rather that their most important interests coincide. Swenson (1989), for example, chronicles conflicts of interest within the LO, the Swedish peak association representing labor, between workers in the traded and non-traded goods sectors. If wages are too high in the industries which do not compete with imports, it drives up the costs for all industries, including those that compete with imports. This can harm economic growth, which, in the long run, will harm wages and employment levels even in the non-traded sectors. Ultimately, to the dismay of workers in these sectors, the LO held down wages in the non-traded sector for precisely this reason. The LO thus minimized rent-seeking by the workers in the non-traded sector, which benefited overall economic growth. High economic growth maximizes aggregate social welfare, even if it harms the short-term interests of workers in the non-traded sectors — which is precisely my point.

peak associations represent persons with like interests,[45] the representatives of geographically-based districts must strive to accomplish the nearly impossible task of representing persons with diverse interests.

The most efficient political organization possible would be one which makes it easy for the government to consult all the relevant information regarding issues it must decide, but one which nonetheless permits that government to reach a timely decision. This is the second component of democratic efficiency. The collection of information would be greatly facilitated by some systematized consultation with the interest groups making up the society, and the ability to come to a decision would be greatly facilitated if there were just a few large groups to consult, rather than hundreds of small groups. The reason is that large groups provide economies of scale with regard to information.

Imagine that the government had to go to the library, rather than to interest groups, to find out the preferences of the people in society. If there were thousands of libraries, each with part of the information, it would take a very long time for the government to collect the necessary information. But if there were just a few libraries, each with a competent and helpful librarian, then the information collection would be a lot easier. Peak associations are the libraries containing the preference information that the government needs. The librarians are the officials of the association with which the government consults.

---

[45] This, of course, assumes that people voluntarily join groups of people with like interests, rather than being forced to join groups of people with dissimilar interests.

The more inclusive are the interest groups that the government consults, the more efficient will be the government's decision-making process. Thus, the degree to which interest groups are centralized in a given society can serve as a measurement of both the equality of the distribution of power in society (the first component of democratic efficiency) and the ability of the government to reach a decision (the second component of democratic efficiency).[46]

I propose that a country's level of democratic efficiency should predict the degree to which government policies (both foreign and domestic) maximize aggregate social welfare.[47] Part I of this book will test this theory with regard to a number of policy outputs, utilizing the two indicators of democratic efficiency discussed above: the distribution of wealth and the centralization of interest groups.

There exist no statistics on the distribution of wealth in most countries. Indeed, wealth is very difficult to calculate. Data are available, however, on the distribution of income[48] for many countries. Wealth and income are not the same, but wealth tends to produce income (and vice versa).

---

[46] One way of measuring the degree of centralization of interest groups would be to employ a Herfindahl index for capital and for labor.

[47] I am concerned with the degree to which government policies maximize aggregate social welfare in the way that a benevolent social planner would. I will measure the degree that this is maximized in terms of comparative cross-national results, rather than analyzing each country in the world, policy-by-policy. For example, I will show that countries with low rates of inequality tend to have higher economic growth rates than countries with high inequality.

[48] For a review of the literature on the relationship between democracy and income inequality, see Sirowy and Inkeles (1990).

Therefore, income data are a good, yet imperfect proxy for data on wealth.

Furthermore, according to Huntington, there is a strong connection between income inequality and the distribution of power:

> Since democracy means, in some measure, majority rule, democracy is only possible if the majority is a relatively satisfied middle class, and not an impoverished majority confronting an inordinately wealthy oligarchy. A substantial middle class, in turn, may be the product of the relatively equal distribution of land in agrarian societies that may otherwise be relatively poor, such as the early nineteenth century United States or twentieth century Costa Rica. It may also be the result of a relatively high level of development, which produces greater income equality in industrial as compared to industrializing societies.[49]

Finally, groups and individuals with a disproportionate share of political power commonly demand tax breaks and subsidies from their governments, redistributing income toward them, and making the distribution of income more unequal. On the other hand, when political power is widely distributed (such as in democratic countries), governments are more likely to redistribute income to the poor, thereby making the distribution of income more equal. Thus, the distribution of income can provide a good indication of the distribution of power in society.

I have used income distribution data compiled by the World Bank to create a Gini index of inequality for each country for which data are available. Given my assumption about the relationship between wealth and political power, I

---

[49] Huntington (1984), p. 413.

have excluded Communist countries, where this relationship should not apply.[50]

Data on interest groups are somewhat easier to come by than data on the distribution of wealth. Ideally, I would compare countries based on the strength and unity of both labor and capital. Unfortunately, for most countries there are no data available regarding the strength and unity of capital. Therefore, I will be using only data on labor union strength and unity for this independent variable. This absence of data on capital is not a fatal flaw, however. One should expect capital to be at least as well organized as labor as it attempts to counterbalance the influence of unions on government policies. I have used a Herfindahl index to calculate the strength and unity of labor in each country for which data are available.

---

[50] In Communist countries, a person's income is not a very good indication of that person's political power. In such countries, government policies are not influenced by the economic clout of individuals, since it is the state, not individuals, that owns the means of production. Similarly, in Communist countries, power is rewarded with greater income to a much smaller degree than in capitalist countries. Status and privilege are more important rewards, given that prices tend to be set by the government at a level below the market clearing level, such that goods are often unavailable at any price. In such a system, an increase in income has little marginal utility. Instead, the politically powerful gain access to special stores, larger apartments, vacation homes, etc. Such differences between capitalist and Communist countries in terms of indicators of the distribution of power make it impossible for me to choose an independent variable relevant to both groups of countries. It is for this reason that I exclude the Communist countries, which are by far the less numerous group.

Independent Variables
(indicators of Democratic Efficiency)
- **Gini Index of Income Inequality**[51]
- **Herfindahl Index of Organized Labor Strength & Unity**[52]

I have used these independent variables to test the relationship between democratic efficiency and a number of indicators of economic performance and efficient government. Each chapter in Part I presents the results of statistical tests using data from a large number of countries. Chapter 2 tests the hypothesis that a given country's level of democratic efficiency is inversely related to the degree to which the government applies fiscal stimuli for short-term electoral gains, resulting in a "political business cycle." Chapter 3 examines the relationship between democratic efficiency and economic growth rates. Chapters 4 and 5 expand the scope

---

[51] My data on the distribution of income within countries come from the World Bank (1979–93). The Gini index, G, is calculated by the following formula:

$$G = 2\sum(x_i - y_i)(\Delta x_i)$$

For any given country, x_i indicates a given quintile group of households (i.e. the poorest 20% of households, the next poorest 20%, etc.) and y_i is the share of total household income received by quintile group i. See Alker (1965), p. 42.

[52] I utilize data on union strength and centralization from *Trade Unions of the World* (various editions). The Herfindahl index is the sum of the squared percentages of the labor force owing allegiance to each union confederation. It ranges from 0 to +1. It is positively related to union density and negatively related to the division of the labor movement among multiple union confederations.

of my analysis into policies having international implications. They consider the relationship between democratic efficiency and, respectively, the level of trade protectionism and the level of military spending.

References

Alchian, Armen A., and Harold Demsetz. 1972. "Production, Information Costs, and Economic Organization." *American Economic Review* 62: 777–795.

Alker, Hayward R., Jr. 1965. *Mathematics and Politics*. New York: Macmillan.

Apter, David E. 1955. *Gold Coast in Transition*. Princeton: Princeton University Press.

Apter, David E. 1973. *Political Change*. London: Frank Cass.

Arat, Zehra F. 1988. "Democracy and Economic Development: Modernization Theory Revisited." *Comparative Politics* 21: 21–36.

Aristotle. 1974. "The Constitution of Athens." In *Aristotle's Constitutions of Athens and Related Texts*, trans. Kurt von Fritz and Ernst Kapp. New York: Hafner Press.

Barro, Robert J. 1991. "Economic Growth in a Cross Section of Countries." *Quarterly Journal of Economics* 106: 407–443.

Becker, Gary S. 1983. "A Theory of Competition among Pressure Groups for Political Influence." *Quarterly Journal of Economics* 98: 371–700.

Becker, Gary S. 1985. "Public Policies, Pressure Groups, and Dead Weight Costs." *Journal of Public Economics* 28: 329–347.

Bollen, Kenneth A. 1980. "Issues in the Comparative Measurement of Political Democracy." *American Sociological Review* 45: 370–390.

Coleman, James S. 1960. "Conclusion: The Political Systems of the Developing Area." In *The Politics of Developing Areas*, ed. Gabriel A. Almond and James S. Coleman. Princeton: Princeton University Press, 532–76.

Consumer Reports. July 1993. "Can You Trust the Graders?" pp. 441–442.

Coulter, P. 1975. *Social Mobilization and Liberal Democracy*. Lexington, MA: Lexington Books.

Crichlow, Joel M. 1988. *An Introduction to Distributed and Parallel Computing*. New York: Prentice Hall.

Dahl, Robert A. 1971. *Polyarchy: Participation and Opposition*. New Haven: Yale University Press.

De Schweinitz, Jr., Karl. 1964. *Industrialization and Democracy*. New York: The Free Press of Glencoe.

Doyle, Michael W. 1986. "Liberalism and World Politics." *American Political Science Review* 80: 1151–69.

Freedom House. 2002. *Freedom in the World Country Ratings*. Freedom House Website: www.freedomhouse.org/ratings/index.htm.

Gore, Al. 1992. *Earth in the Balance: Ecology and the Human Spirit*. New York: Houghton Mifflin.

Huntington, Samuel P. 1984. "Will More Countries Become Democratic?" *Political Science Quarterly* 99: 193–218.

Jackman, Robert W. 1973. "On the Relationship of Economic Development to Political Performance." *American Journal of Political Science* 17: 611–621.

Katzenstein, Peter J. 1985. *Small States in World Markets: Industrial Policy in Europe*. Ithaca, NY: Cornell University Press.

Klein, Benjamin, Robert G. Crawford, and Armen A. Alchian. 1978. "Vertical Integration, Appropriable Rents, and the Competitive Contracting Process." *Journal of Law and Economics* 21: 297–326.

Klein, Burton H. 1959. *Germany's Economic Preparedness for War*. Cambridge, MA: Harvard University Press.

Lake, David A. 1992. "Powerful Pacifists: Democratic States and War." *American Political Science Review* 86: 24–37.

Layne, Christopher. 1994. "Kant or Cant: The Myth of the Democratic Peace." *International Security* 19: 5–49.

Lipset, Seymour Martin. 1960. *Political Man*. New York: Doubleday & Co.

Machiavelli, Niccolo. 1965. "A Discourse on Remodeling the Government of Florence." In *Machiavelli: The Chief Works and Others*, vol. I, trans. Allan Gilbert. Durham, NC: Duke University Press, 101–115.

Maoz, Zeev, and Bruce Russett. 1993. "Normative and Structural Causes of Democratic Peace, 1946–1986." *American Political Science Review* 87: 624–638.

National Public Radio. February 22, 2002 broadcast. "Anthrax Computing."

North, Douglas C. 1981. *Structure and Change In Economic History.* New York: W.W. Norton & Co.

Olson, Mancur. 1982. *The Rise and Decline of Nations: Economic Growth, Stagflation, and Social Rigidities*. New Haven: Yale University Press.

Olson, Mancur. 1993. "Dictatorship, Democracy, and Development." *American Political Science Review* 87: 567–576.

Owen, John M. 1994. "How Liberalism Produces Democratic Peace." *International Security* 19: 87–125.

Przeworski, Adam and Michael Wallerstein. 1988. "The Structural Dependence of the State on Capital." *American Political Science Review* 82: 11–29.

Rasmusen, Eric and J. Mark Ramseyer. 1994. "Cheap Bribes and the Corruption Ban: A Coordination Game Among Rational Legislators." *Public Choice* 78: 305–327.

Schultz, Kenneth A. and Barry R. Weingast. 1994. "The Democratic Advantage: The Institutional Sources of State Power in International Competition." Paper presented at the 1994 meeting of the American Political Science Association.

Schumpeter, Joseph A. 1942. *Capitalism, Socialism, and Democracy*. New York: Harper and Row.

Sharp, John A. 1987. *An Introduction to Distributed and Parallel Processing*. Oxford: Blackwell Scientific Publications.

Sirowy, Larry, and Alex Inkeles. 1990. "The Effects of Democracy on Economic Growth and Inequality: A Review." *Studies in Comparative Economic Development* 25: 126–157.

Spiro, David E. 1994. "The Insignificance of the Liberal Peace." *International Security* 19: 50–86.

Swenson, Peter. 1989. *Fair Shares: Unions, Pay, and Politics in Sweden and West Germany*. Ithaca, NY: Cornell University Press.

Trade Unions of the World. 1st Ed. (1987), 2nd Ed. (1989), and 3rd Ed. (1992). London: Longman International Reference.

Tiebout, Charles M. 1956. "A Pure Theory of Local Expenditures." *Journal of Political Economy* 64: 416–424.

Tilly, Charles. 1990. *Coercion, Capital, and European States, A.D. 990–1990*. Oxford: Basil Blackwell.

United States. October 31, 1945. *The Effects of Strategic Bombing on the German War Economy*. The United States Strategic Bombing Survey, Overall Economic Effects Division.

Varian, Hal R. 1990. *Intermediate Microeconomics*. New York: W.W. Norton & Co.

Webster's Ninth New Collegiate Dictionary. 1985. Springfield, MA: Merriam-Webster.

Williamson, Oliver E. 1985. *The Economic Institutions of Capitalism*. New York: The Free Press.

Wittman, Donald. 1989. "Why Democracies Produce Efficient Results." *Journal of Political Economy* 97: 1395–1424.

World Bank. 1979 edition through 1995 edition. *World Development Report*. Oxford: Oxford University Press.

World Bank. 2002. World Development Indicators Database. World Bank Website: www.worldbank.org/data/quickreference/quickref.html

2

Political Business Cycles

Review of the literature

Since the 1970s, political scientists and economists have studied what has become known as the political business cycle. Various scholars have presented evidence that government policies significantly affect macroeconomic indicators.[1] Two types of political business cycles have emerged: "ideological cycles" and "opportunistic cycles."[2] Ideological cycles manifest themselves when inflation rises and unemployment falls under left-wing governments, and vice versa under right-wing governments.[3] Opportunistic cycles occur when incum-

---

[1] Schneider and Frey (1988) and Nordhaus (1989) present comprehensive surveys of the political business cycle literature.

[2] I borrow these terms from Nordhaus (1989).

[3] There is a large literature on ideological cycles. Hibbs (1977, 1982, 1987) is considered an authority on the subject. Alesina and Roubini

bent executives employ fiscal and/or monetary policy in efforts to create economic conditions which make voters more likely to re-elect them.[4] This chapter will show that the severity of a country's opportunistic political business cycle is negatively related to that country's level of democratic efficiency.

Theorists of the opportunistic political business cycle claim that voters are more likely to vote for the incumbent party if good economic conditions prevail on election day. Incumbent presidents and prime ministers are aware of this, and employ various mechanisms to put more money into the pockets of voters and/or to stimulate the economy during the months preceding an election. Politicians also try to delay

---

(1992), Alt (1985), Alt and Chrystal (1983), Nordhaus (1989), and Tufte (1978) all examine both ideological and opportunistic cycles.

[4] Nordhaus (1975) launched the study of opportunistic cycles. Other studies finding evidence of opportunistic cycles include Alt (1985), Haynes and Stone (1988), Keil (1988), Maloney and Smirlock (1981), and Tufte (1978). Nordhaus (1989) extends and reaffirms his earlier conclusions, but his view of the irrationality of voters is attacked by Alesina in his commentary. Rogoff and Sibert (1988) offer a formal model of an opportunistic cycle based on rational voter behavior and information asymmetries. Alesina and Roubini (1992) find that inflation increases after elections and Alesina, Cohen, and Roubini (1992) find evidence of "loose" fiscal and monetary policy preceding elections, but argue that these results are consistent with rational voter behavior. Alt and Chrystal (1983) criticize much of the political business cycles literature. They claim that the empirical evidence in support of Nordhaus' (1975) model is weak. While admitting that Tufte (1978) presents some convincing evidence, they also criticize the fact that disposable income does not rise in all election years. To be fair to Tufte, one must note that he admits that, for ideological or other reasons, a particular government sometimes refuses to manipulate economic policy for short-term political gain. The fact that governments do so as often as they do makes Tufte's work interesting in its own right.

the cost of such actions until after the election. In general, governments tend to cut taxes, increase spending, and raise social welfare benefits just before an election, and to do the reverse after the election. Many scholars claim that governments systematically engage in contractionary fiscal and/or monetary policies early in their terms, causing unemployment to rise and inflation to decline, and to engage in expansionary policies in the months preceding an election, causing unemployment to fall by election day. Such expansionary policies result in a surge of inflation, which must be cured, once again, with contractionary policies after the election is over.

Such politically-induced boom and bust cycles cannot but be harmful to a country's economy. They represent a misallocation of resources that should lessen long-term economic growth. If pre-election fiscal stimulus was not excessive, it would not be associated with a post-election inflation surge. If stimulus is economically justified, it is hard to explain why it is so much more prevalent just before elections. Governments certainly can impact inflation and unemployment levels in an economy. Keynesian economists argue that such government manipulation of the economy may sometimes be beneficial at correcting market failures. But no economist would argue that such manipulation is beneficial to the economy when done for purely political purposes.

Most studies of political business cycles examine the coincidence of elections with changes in inflation and unemployment rates. Governments have the ability to impact these statistics to some degree. But exogenous shocks to the economy arguably have a much greater impact. Indeed, major events such as a rise in oil prices or a global recession can easily mask the impact on unemployment and inflation rates of a government's pre-election manipulations. This is not to say that these manipulations do not have any effect on voters, but rather, that it may be better to examine a more direct effect of these manipulations than the rates of inflation and unemployment. After all, a voter is more likely to be affected by a change in his/her own family's income than by changes in the overall inflation or unemployment rate.

Furthermore, only a very unsophisticated government can be expected to try to influence the election returns solely by increasing spending in the hopes of lowering the unemployment rate. It takes a very long time for money to cycle through the economy to the point at which it creates new jobs. It is more likely for the government to cut individual income taxes and/or to increase the transfer payments that it disperses to individuals. This may lower unemployment in the long term. But in the short term it certainly puts more money in the pockets of voters. Tufte (1978) shows that the U.S. government systematically increased social security and veterans benefits just before elections in the 1960s and 1970s. He also shows that the yearly peaks for government transfer payments occur just before the election in election years, but that in non-election years they tend to peak in December.[5]

Such patterns seem to indicate that the U.S. government was trying to put more money in the voters' pockets just before the election.[6] Acceleration in real income growth should reflect this more directly than a drop in the unem-

---

[5] Tufte (1978), chapter 2.

[6] One recent and innovative example of this was when President George Bush reduced the federal withholding from paychecks before the 1992 election. Many voters were unpleasantly surprised to find out the fol-

ployment rate. Tufte finds that in nineteen of twenty-seven democracies, the rate of real income growth was more likely to increase in election than in non-election years.[7] Powell (1982) attempts to explain why this did not occur in more countries. He shows that the extent of a political business cycle, as measured by Tufte, depends upon a country's constitutional and electoral system. Presidential systems and parliamentary systems that produce single party majorities tend to have strong political business cycles, parliamentary systems that sometimes produce majority governments have weaker cycles, whereas other systems tend not to exhibit much, if any, sign of a political business cycle.[8]

Powell speculates that political business cycles occur less frequently when there is a coalition government than when a single party controls the executive branch because it is difficult to get a coalition to agree to manipulate the economy for electoral purposes. This may be so. But it raises an interesting question with regard to democratic efficiency: Do constitutional arrangements that limit the concentration of executive power lead to greater democratic efficiency, thereby making a political business cycle less likely? Or, conversely, does a high level of democratic efficiency allow a country to adopt institutions characterized by a sharing of executive power, thereby making a political business cycle less likely?

---

lowing spring that not enough money had been withheld from their paychecks, meaning that they owed the government money, rather than being owed a tax refund.

[7] Tufte (1978), Table 1–1, p. 12.

[8] Powell (1982), pp. 208–212.

This "chicken or egg" problem could perhaps be solved by an examination of whether democratic efficiency was unusually high before countries adopted constitutional changes making coalition governments more likely, or whether increases in democratic efficiency followed such constitutional changes. Either way, however, democratic efficiency plays a vital role in explaining the comparative severity of political business cycles. In Powell's sample, those countries which tend to have the weakest political business cycles also tend to be those countries with the least income inequality and the strongest labor movements, both of which are indicators of democratic efficiency. Furthermore, countries characterized by coalition governments tend to be those with proportional representation. Electoral systems of this sort tend to produce multiple parties with distinct ideologies. The less ideologically distinct are political parties, the more impact government economic manipulations should have on the voter. Barring ideological alternatives, the state of the economy and of family finances remain some of the few bases by which voters can choose between competing parties. Indeed, as I have suggested in Chapter 1,[9] interest representation (by peak associations or through proportional representation) is superior to geographic representation (single member district plurality systems) at representing the preferences of society and at facilitating efficient government decision-making. As Anthony Downs (1957) points out, single member district plurality electoral systems tend to result

---

[9] See p. 36.

in political systems dominated by two parties whose policy positions are not significantly different from one another.

Democratic Efficiency

Democratic efficiency indicates policymaking that maximizes aggregate social welfare. The misallocation of economic resources caused by a government for partisan political reasons harms long-term economic growth. This deviates from the maximization of aggregate social welfare, and therefore should be correlated with a low level of democratic efficiency. In addition, such manipulations are a waste of taxpayers' money. Money spent on manipulating elections serves no purpose that is beneficial to society. It could have been spent on something that benefited society at large or the economy as a whole. It could even have been given away to special interest groups which lobby the government for subsidies. But instead it was spent such that incumbent politicians were the main beneficiaries. This alone should arouse the indignation of voters, to the extent that their country's level of democratic efficiency allows.

Misallocations of resources in the economy generally make the distribution of wealth and income more unequal. This harms society in general, but it harms the less well off more than others. The more equal is the distribution of wealth, the more of a stake the average citizen has in the overall health of the economy. Thus, the more economic equality there is in society, the more society should resist the rent-seeking behavior of politicians, that is, resist the attempts of politicians to manipulate the economy for their own short-term benefit. The more united and encompassing is the labor movement, the more the overall health of the economy should matter to the labor movement. Also, the more powerful is labor, the better able it should be to resist government policies that harm the economy and thereby harm the interests of labor. Thus, the more united and encompassing is the labor movement, the less severe the political business cycle should be.

I propose to test these two hypotheses. Tufte (1978) presents data comparing the increase in real disposable income in election years and non-election years. Powell (1982) uses the difference between these two figures as his dependent variable, which he explains by differences in constitutional and electoral systems. I propose to employ my two indicators of democratic efficiency, the Gini index of income inequality and the Herfindahl index of labor movement strength/unity, as the independent variables. I expect to find a negative relationship between democratic efficiency and the severity of the political business cycle.

Empirical Evidence

I have constructed an index with which to compare the magnitude of political business cycles cross-nationally. Tufte (1978) presents data on the number of election years and non-election years, 1961–72, in which the rate of growth of real disposable income increased.[10] I extend the years of coverage to 1982.[11] For the period 1961–1982, I calculate the percentage of election years in which the growth rate of real disposable income increased. I also calculate the percentage of non-election years in which the rate of growth

---

[10] Tufte (1978), Table 1–1.
[11] Like Tufte, I rely upon OECD (1985) data for disposable income. Leonard and Natkiel (1987) provide data on election years.

of real disposable income increased. The magnitude of the political business cycle is the difference between the two. The larger is this difference, the greater the magnitude of the political business cycle. This is my dependent variable.

For my independent variables, I employ a Gini index of income inequality, a Herfindahl index of labor strength and unity, and an ordinal variable representing the five constitutional/electoral categories that Powell (1982) employs. Both the Gini and Herfindahl data are based on measurements for specific years, and the measured years differ from country to country. For several countries, I have a Gini or Herfindahl index for several different years during the period 1961–1982. In such cases, I employ the average of these multiple values.

Powell (1982) groups countries into five categories, based on constitutional characteristics (presidential system, parliamentary system, or Swiss-style collective executive system) and electoral outcomes (always a coalition or minority government, mixed electoral outcome, or always a single-party majority government). He finds no evidence of a political business cycle in collective executive systems, and in general, the severity of the political business cycle bears a direct relationship with the degree to which the governments tend to exhibit majoritarian tendencies.[12] I used an ordinal variable numbered from 0 to 5, representing the ranked severity of political business cycle associated with each of Powell's categories.[13]

---

[12] See Powell (1982), pp. 208–212.

[13] 0=collective executive, 1=always coalition or minority government (parliamentary), 2=mixed electoral outcomes (parliamentary), 3=presidential system, 4=always a single party majority (parliamentary). I use Powell's (1982) codings for the countries in my sample.

I find that democratic efficiency does indeed have a negative relationship with the magnitude of the political business cycle. As Table 2 shows, each indicator of democratic efficiency is significantly related to the magnitude of a country's political business cycle. Figures 2.1 and 2.2 graphically illustrate that income inequality is positively related to the magnitude of a country's political business cycle, while labor power is negatively related. A 10 percentage point increase in income inequality results in a 14 percentage point increase in the magnitude of the political business cycle. Similarly, a 10 percentage point increase in labor strength/ unity results in a 31 percentage point decrease in the severity of the political business cycle.

The inclusion of the indicators of democratic efficiency substantially increases the explanatory power of Powell's model. Using only the constitutional/electoral outcome data as the independent variable, $R^2=0.42$; when the indicators of democratic efficiency are included, the R^2 rises to 0.71.

Conclusions

There exists a political business cycle in most OECD countries. The magnitude of this cycle varies considerably, however, from one country to the next. Powell (1982) shows that institutional factors help to explain these differences. I show that democratic efficiency substantially increases the explanatory value of Powell's model. I find that the higher a country's level of democratic efficiency, the weaker its political business cycle tends to be.

References

Alesina, Alberto, Gerald D. Cohen, and Nouriel Roubini. 1992. "Macroeconomic Policy and Elections in OECD Democracies." *Economics and Politics* 4: 1–30.

Alesina, Alberto, and Nouriel Roubini. 1992. "Political Cycles in OECD Economies." *Review of Economic Studies* 59: 663–668.

Alt, James E. 1985. "Political Parties, World Demand, and Unemployment: Domestic and International Sources of Economic Activity." *American Political Science Review* 79: 1016–1040.

Alt, James E., and K. Alec Chrystal. 1983. *Political Economics*. Berkeley: University of California Press.

Downs, Anthony. 1957. *An Economic Theory of Democracy*. Boston: Addison Wesley.

Haynes, Stephen E., and Joe Stone. 1988. "Does the Political Business Cycle Dominate U.S. Unemployment and Inflation. Some New Evidence." In *Political Business Cycles*, ed. Thomas D. Willett. Durham, NC: Duke University Press, 276–293.

Hibbs, Douglas A., Jr. 1987. *The American Political Economy: Macroeconomics and Electoral Politics in Contemporary America*. Cambridge, MA: Harvard University Press.

Hibbs, Douglas A. Jr. 1982. "Economic Outcomes and Political Support for British Governments among Occupational Classes: A Dynamic Analysis." *American Political Science Review* 76: 259–279.

Hibbs, Douglas A. Jr. 1977. "Political Parties and Macroeconomic Policy." *American Political Science Review* 71: 1467–1487.

Keil, Manfred W. 1988. "Is the Political Business Cycle Really Dead?" *Southern Economic Journal* 55: 86–99.

Leonard, Dick, and Richard Natkiel. 1987. *The Economist World Atlas of Elections*. London: Hodder and Stoughton.

Maloney, Kevin J., and Michael L. Smirlock. 1981. "Business Cycles and the Political Process." *Southern Economic Journal* 48: 377–392.

Nordhaus, William D. 1989. "Alternative Approaches to the Political Business Cycle." *Brookings Papers on Economic Activity* 2: 1–68.

Nordhaus, William D. 1975. "The Political Business Cycle." *Review of Economic Studies* 42: 169–190.

OECD. 1985. *National Accounts Statistics*. Paris: Organization of Economic Cooperation and Development.

Powell, G. Bingham, Jr. 1982. *Contemporary Democracies.* Cambridge, MA: Harvard University Press.

Rogoff, Kenneth, and Anne Sibert. 1988. "Elections and Macroeconomic Policy Cycles." *Review of Economic Studies* 55: 1–16.

Schneider, Friedrich, and Bruno Frey. 1988. "Politico-Economic Models of Macroeconomic Policy: A Review of the Empirical Evidence." In *Political Business Cycles,* ed. Thomas D. Willett. Durham, NC: Duke University Press, 239–275.

Tufte, Edward R. 1978. *Political Control of the Economy.* Princeton: Princeton University Press.

Table 2

Dependent Variable
- Political business cycle magnitude[14]

Independent Variable	Coefficient	T-statistic
• Constitutional/electoral[15]	0.069	3.3

N=17
R^2=0.42
Adj. R^2=0.38

Dependent Variable
- Political business cycle magnitude

Independent Variables	Coefficient	T-statistic
• Income inequality[16]	1.4	1.3
• Labor strength & unity[17]	−3.1	−2.5
• Constitutional/electoral	0.055	3.3

N=17
R^2=0.71
Adj. R^2=0.65

---

[14] See p. 56.
[15] See note 13 above.
[16] Gini index. For formula and sources of data, see chap. 1, note 51.
[17] Herfindahl index. For formula and sources of data, see chap. 1, note 52.

Dependent Variable
- Political business cycle magnitude

Independent Variable	*Coefficient*	*T-statistic*
• Income Inequality	3.4	2.7

N=17
R^2=0.33
Adj. R^2=0.28

Dependent Variable
- Political business cycle magnitude

Independent Variable	*Coefficient*	*T-statistic*
• Labor strength & unity	–4.48	–2.9

N=17
R^2=0.35
Adj. R^2=0.31

Figure 2.1

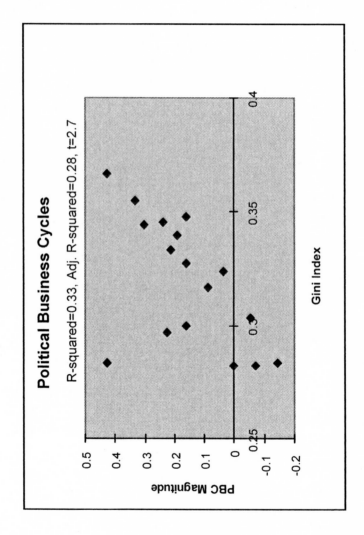

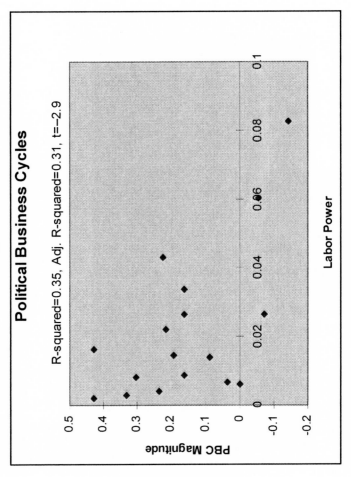

Figure 2.2

Political Business Cycles

R-squared=0.35, Adj. R-squared=0.31, t=-2.9

3

Economic Growth

Since the 18th century, the number of democratic countries in the world has increased rapidly. This rising tide of democracy has paralleled the most rapid expansion of human wealth and standards of living in the history of civilization. The first modern democratic states took root at the beginnings of the Industrial Revolution. Democracy prospered and spread as the economic growth created by this revolution expanded. Indeed, virtually all of the fifty richest countries in the world today are democracies.[1] Just as remarkably, non-democratic countries like South Korea and Taiwan have become more democratic as they have developed economically.

Democratic countries tend to be the richest countries in the world on a per capita basis. The only way that

---

[1] See p. 8.

they could have achieved this distinction was to experience economic growth rates higher than those of non-democratic countries. This chapter will explore the connection between democratic efficiency and a country's rate of economic growth.

Gross domestic product (GDP), the value of all goods and services produced in a given country's economy, indicates the size of that economy. Thus, GDP growth indicates an increase in the size of the economy. One can represent this process mathematically with the following Cobb-Douglas production function:

$$Y = AK^{\alpha}L^{\beta}: \alpha, \beta \in (0,1)$$

where Y is GDP, A is total factor productivity, K is capital, and L is labor. Thus, Y increases (economic growth occurs) when (1) there is an increase in the amount of labor in the economy, (2) there is an increase in the amount of capital (investment) in the economy, or (3) the productivity of labor and/or capital increases.

This chapter argues that the third determinant of economic growth is primarily responsible for the superior economic performance of democracies. More specifically, democratic governments tend to place fewer constraints on innovation than do non-democratic governments. It is innovation which increases the total factor productivity, and thus economic growth. Furthermore, an increase in total factor productivity has a multiplier effect on economic growth rates by attracting new labor and capital. If the marginal productivity of labor and capital increases, the marginal revenue earned from these factors increases as well (wages and the return on investment capital increases), spurring an influx of these two factors. Labor flows into the economy (or, when there are restrictions on immigration, labor market participation increases) and so does investment. This chapter will show that democratic efficiency bears a positive relationship with total factor productivity, and that total factor productivity is primarily responsible for the economic superiority of democracies. Furthermore, I will argue that this relationship intensifies as a country develops economically, because human capital becomes increasingly important to economic growth at higher levels of development.

I will develop this argument more fully below. But first, I will provide a brief survey of the literature on the relationship between democracy and economic growth.

Review of the literature

Many theorists of comparative politics have claimed that economic development (the result of economic growth) causes democracy. For example, Seymour M. Lipset describes economic development as "requisite" to democracy.[2] More recently, Robert Dahl (1989) has claimed that economic development spreads economic power—and thus political aspirations—among increasing numbers of people, thereby fostering democracy. Statistical studies since the 1970s have found a strong association between economic growth and democracy.[3]

---

[2] Lipset (1959). See also chapter 2 of Lipset (1960). De Schweinitz (1964) claims that economic development is a necessary but not a sufficient condition for the development of democracy.

[3] Jackman (1973), Bollen (1979, 1983), Bollen and Jackman (1985), Brunk, Caldeira, and Lewis-Beck (1987), and Helliwell (1994) all perform regression-based analyses which find that economic development bears a strong statistically significant relationship with democracy. Arat (1988) and Gonick and Rosh (1988), however, do not find a strong statis-

A correlation between democracy and economic growth implies nothing about causality, however. Does growth lead to democracy, as Lipset and Dahl argue, or is it the reverse?[4] The answer is far from simple. First of all, contemporary definitions of democracy often encompass a number of economic, civil, and political freedoms. Which type of freedom is responsible for the economic growth associated with democracy? One recent study[5] uses an econometric technique to test the direction of causality. It finds that economic freedom increases economic growth. So do civil and political freedoms.[6] This explains why some non-democratic capitalist countries (notably several in East Asia) have been able to achieve high levels of economic growth without much political freedom. It also helps to explain why some democratic countries like India, where the government has strictly controlled economic activity, have not experienced high growth rates. The question remains, however, why most authoritarian governments blessed with high economic growth rates feel compelled to enlarge the scope of political

---

tical relationship. But Burkhart and Lewis-Beck (1994) point out methodological weaknesses in these two studies. Their own study corrects for these weaknesses and confirms that democracy is strongly associated with economic growth.

[4] Sirowy and Inkeles (1990) provide a good survey of the literature on whether democracy helps or harms economic growth. More recent contributions are discussed below.

[5] Bhalla (1994).

[6] Burkhart and Lewis-Beck (1994) and Helliwell (1994) find that economic development causes democracy, but not vice versa. One possible reason for these conflicting results is that the Gastil democracy index that they employ does not differentiate between political and economic freedoms, as does Bhalla's index.

freedoms as their countries reach higher levels of economic development. As I will soon demonstrate, the answer is that democracy makes economic growth easier in general, and that democracy is necessary for growth to continue at higher levels of development.

But first I should examine the mechanism by which democracy results in a higher economic growth rate. As the Cobb-Douglas production function indicates, economic growth can occur due to an increase in labor, capital, or total factor productivity. Dani Rodrik (1994) demonstrates, for example, that it was an increase in capital (partially due to an increase in savings rates), rather than total factor productivity, which was responsible for the impressive level of economic growth in Taiwan and South Korea since the late 1960s. Paul Krugman (1994) makes the same point with regard to Singapore. Taiwan and South Korea, however, have only been democracies since the late 1980s, and Singapore still is not very democratic.

Mancur Olson (1993) argues that the same mechanism is responsible for the economic superiority of democracies. Olson's theory is that democracies experience superior levels of economic growth because they experience higher levels of investment than non-democracies. This is because democratic governments are able to provide stronger guarantees of property rights than dictatorships. A person is unlikely to invest if s/he cannot expect to derive any personal benefit from such investment. On the other hand, if the law of the land guarantees that the return from one's investments will not be arbitrarily expropriated, there is an incentive for investment, and increased investment will increase economic growth.

Olson explains this in terms of (1) differences in the interests of democratic and non-democratic governments and (2) the greater credibility of democratic institutions. First of all, dictators tend to extract so much revenue from society that they harm economic activity. Dictators behave just like any other special interest: they attempt to maximize their own income even to the detriment of the society at large. Rational dictators will extract much higher levels of taxes and bribes than rational democratic leaders. This is because the income maximizing tax rate for the dictator, like the profit-maximizing price of the monopolist, is higher than would be optimal for society. The optimal tax rate for society would lie where the marginal benefit of government services equals the marginal deadweight cost of the tax. The income-maximizing tax rate[7] for the dictator, however, is the rate at which marginal tax revenue equal marginal cost in terms of taxes lost due to a slowdown in economic activity. Since tax revenues go into the dictator's pocket, s/he will raise the tax rate to the point at which the economy will shrink so much due to a further tax increase that tax revenues would actually go down. A rational dictator, therefore, sets the tax rate so high that it severely retards economic growth.[8]

Democratic leaders cannot set the tax rate this high. Elected officials who try to soak society by raising taxes

---

[7] In this sense, the extraction of bribes can be considered a form of taxation. Like taxes, it imposes additional costs on economic activity and retards economic growth. Unlike taxes, however, bribes almost never pay for the provision of public goods.

[8] This is an elegant theory, but as I mentioned above, Singapore, South Korea and Taiwan are major exceptions.

higher than the optimal rate will face the wrath of the voters.[9]

Secondly, dictatorships discourage investment because the credibility of property rights protections under dictatorships is always suspect. Since the law is what the dictator says it is, any guarantees of property rights are held hostage to the whim of the dictator. Guarantees of property rights are only as strong as the word of the dictator. Democratic countries, on the other hand, usually impose severe roadblocks in the way of those who would infringe upon property rights. For example, democratic counties often tie the hands of policymakers in this regard by vesting an independent judiciary with the power to strike down laws which infringe upon fundamental property rights[10] and/or by making their central banks independent of political authorities.[11] Finally,

---

[9] By the same token, as Rasmusen and Ramseyer (1994) demonstrate, democratic legislators accept much lower bribes than dictators. In this case, bribery could be considered an indirect form of taxation. See Chapter 1.

[10] Many democracies (such as the United States, Canada, Germany, France, and Italy) have an independent judiciary empowered to protect property rights through judicial review. Most democracies which do not have such an institution are subject to the power of the European Court of Justice (ECJ), which performs the same role throughout the European Union as a whole (although access to the ECJ tends to be more limited than to national courts).

[11] Independent central banks limit the spending power of governments by counteracting inflationary fiscal policy with strict monetary policy. They thus protect property rights by limiting the power of governments to use inflation as an indirect tax on capital. For an examination of the political process leading to central bank independence, see Goodman (1991); Alesina and Summers (1991) provide an interesting analysis of the economic impact of central bank independence.

even a benevolent dictator who vigilantly protects property rights cannot guarantee the continuation of such policies under the rule of his/her successor. This certainly can make investors wary.[12]

Critique of Olson's Theory

Olson provides an elegant explanation as to why democracies tend to experience higher levels of economic growth than non-democracies. But his model leaves many questions unanswered. First of all, there are many empirical examples that do not fit Olson's theory, such as the investment-led growth in non-democratic Taiwan and South Korea in the 1970s. Why didn't these countries' dictators milk their countries dry, as so many did elsewhere?

Secondly, Olson does not convincingly explain how dictatorships develop into democracies. He argues that democracy develops from dictatorship either when it is imposed from the outside or when no leader internally is strong enough to seize all power for him/herself. Some democracies certainly did arise under such circumstances, but many others did not. What is the reason for such "anomalous" democratization?

Thirdly, Olson takes for granted that democratic governments will always adopt secure protection of property rights. He does not explain why democratic countries

---

[12]A good example of this was the increasing flight of human and investment capital from Hong Kong as the date for the colony's return to Communist China approached. This occurred despite the Chinese government's assurances that they would not interfere with Hong Kong's political and economic processes after gaining sovereignty over the island.

choose to limit the power of their governments by imposing superpolitical safeguards of property rights. Olson's hypothetical democratic leader, unlike a dictator, is constrained from using taxes to line his/her own pockets. But what is to stop a leftist democratic leader from expropriating all of the property of the rich and redistributing it to the poor?

The problem with Olson's theory is that it overlooks the interrelationship between labor, capital, and total factor productivity. While it may be true that strong protection of property rights provides an incentive for investment by lowering the *risk* of expropriation, so does an increase in total factor productivity, since it increases the *return* on investment. If the democratic economic advantage is superior total factor productivity growth, rather than just higher levels of investment, then investment-led growth in Singapore, Taiwan, and South Korea no longer undermines the democracy-growth argument. These countries merely may be taking advantage of a different avenue of growth (high levels of investment) from the one in which democracies are particularly advantaged (high levels of innovation). Or, on the other hand, perhaps it is not democracy, *per se*, but democratic efficiency that results in higher levels of both investment and innovation. I will consider both of these possibilities in turn.

First of all, how can total factor productivity increase? In the case of capital, the answer is innovation. Innovation could be technological or organizational. Technological innovation, in fact, is given impetus by the very protection of property rights that Olson lauds. Douglas North (1981) chronicles how the development of property rights throughout history spurred the development of new technology and economic growth.

Organizational innovation tends to be spurred by competition. Managers often are content to do things the same way as long as there is no pressure to change. Industry in the former Soviet Union had abundant capital and a highly educated workforce, but a dearth of innovation due to lack of competition. The economic growth rate gap between East and West after the 1960s resulted largely from increases in total factor productivity in the West. Massive investment can spur economic growth rates in the short run. But it cannot increase the productivity of capital. Only innovation can do this.

The more capital that is introduced into the economy, the more the marginal return on additional investment decreases. Investment-led growth strategies can create a temporary spurt of economic growth, as occurred in the Soviet Union in the 1950s and 1960s, but eventually growth will stall due to the declining marginal productivity of capital. Diminishing returns can only be transformed into increasing returns through innovation, which is the essence of total factor productivity growth.[13] It is in this sense that Bhalla's (1994) attention to economic freedom is crucial to economic growth.[14]

Labor productivity also can be increased by organizational innovation.[15] It is driven by the same force as the organizational innovation of capital: competition. Again, economic freedom increases economic growth.

---

[13] See Krugman (1994).

[14] I will address the importance of political freedom below.

[15] If this were not the case, management consultancy might not be such a booming industry.

Labor productivity also increases as workers become more skilled. Economic freedom provides incentives for workers to increase their education and skill levels. As long as there is a market that rewards skills and knowledge with higher pay and advancement, human capital will accumulate.

This concept provides a more powerful explanation than Olson's as to why dictatorships develop into democracies. Economic development leads to democracy because, as development proceeds, human capital becomes increasingly important to economic growth. At lower levels of development, most of the advances in productivity occur through increased investment in physical capital. Industrialization can proceed in the early stages with advanced machinery and backward workers. But for development to advance, larger and larger amounts of capital must be invested in people.[16] Increasingly, economic growth depends on the skills of managers, entrepreneurs, and professionals. A middle class develops economic importance.

Several economists have established a strong link between human capital, income distribution, and economic growth.[17] They have found that economic growth is dependent upon the growth of human capital, which is in turn dependent upon the distribution of income (particularly the share of the middle class). This relationship becomes stronger at higher levels of development.

---

[16] Barro (1991) demonstrates that the growth rate of real per capital GDP is positively related to the level of human capital in a given country. Rodrik (1994) emphasizes the highly educated and skilled workforces in South Korea and Taiwan as the primary reasons for the high economic growth rates experienced by these countries since the late 1960s.

[17] Galor and Zeira (1993), Perotti (1992 and 1993), and Persson and Tabellini (1991).

As new people begin to play a greater role in the economy, they amass the power to demand a greater say in how it is run. As I pointed out in Chapter 1, governments either can help or hinder economic growth. Those individuals who can be helped or harmed by government policies can be expected to have an intense interest in the nature of those policies. It is like the metaphor of the software and the trucking company discussed in Chapter 1.[18] The less based in physical capital and the more dependent on human capital is economic growth, the more incentive the investors have to demand voting control. All citizens are, in a sense, stockholders in the economy.[19]

---

[18] See p. 9.

[19] One might argue that citizens are both workers and stockholders, that is, a democracy is like a worker-owned firm. Williamson (1985) discusses the benefits and drawbacks of worker ownership (pp. 265–268). The major benefit, he contends, is that such firms have the potential for earning higher profits, since their workers are willing to work for lower wages (this is what they pay for the luxury of worker control). Williamson also cites several drawbacks to worker ownership: it is harder for them than for capitalist firms to raise capital (since workers in worker-owned firms do not wish to relinquish voting control); good managers tend to leave the firm for higher-paying jobs in capitalist firms; and they tend to degenerate into capitalist enterprise (because greedy founders do not wish to share the benefits with newcomers). Democracies, however, seem to avoid the pitfalls of worker-ownership. As I discussed above, strong property rights protection actually makes it easier for them to raise capital than for non-democracies. Nationalism and other emotional factors tend to prevent successful politicians ("managers") from leaving to run other countries. And relatively low levels of immigration tend to prevent the problem of the greedy founders. (They, for the most part, pass the country on to their own descendants.)

If people are repressed, they will not work as hard and economic growth will lessen.[20] The invisible hand works better than the visible fist. They also will transfer their liquid and human capital overseas if given the chance. Throughout the world, people with money to invest are inclined to send it to financial institutions located in democratic countries such as Switzerland and the United States. In addition, the much maligned "brain drain" from the Third World to the First World is, for the most part, a flow of human capital (skilled professionals) from dictatorships to democracies.

The failures of Communism aptly illustrate that economic repression limits economic growth. But if people are given economic freedom, they will amass economic power that will undermine the political power of the dictator. In a capitalist economy, economic power is the basis of political power. With economic development, new people amass economic power and, eventually, the dictator has to choose between economic growth and a monopoly on political power. If the dictator waits too long, economic development will erode his/her monopoly on political power. If the dictator chooses economic repression, the political system eventually will

---

[20] Eggertsson (1990) illustrates this in his discussion of slavery and sharecropping. See, especially, pages 203–213. Free workers internalize their entire marginal products, whereas slaves and sharecroppers receive only a fraction of their marginal products in compensation. Repressed workers have little incentive to work hard, since an increase in effort provides little, if any, reward. Instead, they can only be induced to work through repression, which causes enormous incentives for shirking. Workers in repressive societies face similar disincentives against hard work and innovation, because in the absence of strong and strictly-enforced property rights, there is a great chance that the authorities will confiscate the benefits of hard work and innovation.

collapse due to economic pressure, just as it did in all of the Communist states in the former Soviet empire.

My third criticism of Olson's theory is that it fails to explain why democratic leaders choose to limit their own power when it comes to control over property rights. Since property rights are crucial to economic growth, the public often demands superpolitical safeguards for property rights as protection against politicians (and voters) with short time horizons. Rational voters demand government policies that balance current personal income for the voters (in terms of redistributionary policies) and long-term economic growth.[21] Rather than confiscating and redistributing all productive non-human capital and bringing the economy to a standstill, even rational poor voters should be expected to prefer redistributionary policies that will permit economic progress to continue.[22] Kydland and Prescott (1977) illustrate this as a differential game between workers and capitalists:

> A majority group, say, the workers, who control the policy might rationally choose to have a constitution which limits their power, say, to expropriate the wealth of the capitalist class. Those with lower discount rates will save more if they know

---

[21] Granted, there is a learning curve in many cases. But even in Argentina and Brazil, where *daily* inflation rates used to rival annual rates in other countries, voters have elected fiscally responsible governments that have slashed budget deficits and brought inflation down to reasonable levels.
[22] Roemer (1995) presents a model which explains why the poor do not expropriate the rich in a 2-party system. He demonstrates that, as long as there exists a second politically salient issue in addition to income redistribution, the party of the left will have to moderate its demands for redistribution in order to satisfy the interests of voters who care about this other issue.

that their wealth will not be expropriated in the future, thereby increasing the marginal product and therefore wages and lowering the price of capital.[23]

In the few cases where parties representing the working class have won a majority in democratic elections, such as in the United Kingdom and Sweden, these parties, once in power, have not tried to destroy capitalism. Instead, they merely have siphoned off a greater share of the income produced under capitalism to fund redistributionary policies under the guise of the welfare state.[24] Taking everything now leaves nothing for the future. Democracy forces people to think about the future.

One added benefit of tying the hands of policymakers is that democratic countries are perceived as better credit

---

[23] Kydland and Prescott (1977), p. 486. One may wonder how it can be rational for a majority to agree to set up an independent central bank or to establish constitutional protections of property rights because such decisions permanently limit the power of the majority. It is rational, however, for a person to "bind" him/herself to a particular future course of action if s/he is uncertain whether s/he will be able to make a rational choice in the future. Elster (1979) calls it "imperfect rationality" to commit oneself in the present to insure against future irrationality. (It is "imperfect" because, although rational at the time of decision, the decisionmaker will be unable to make a rational choice in the future.) He gives the example of Ulysses having himself bound to the mast of his ship before coming within earshot of the island of the Sirens, because he knows that he will be unable to resist their deadly call.

[24] Indeed, Przeworski and Wallerstein (1988) demonstrate that the rate of taxation on consumption can be at virtually any level below 100% without causing a decline in investment. This means that the level of income redistribution and the size of the welfare state can be enormous without harming economic growth, as is empirically demonstrated by the Swedish case.

risks. Democratic governments historically have been able to borrow money at significantly lower interest rates than non-democratic governments.[25] This has enhanced the economic growth of democracies in two ways. First of all, lower interest rates mean that it is cheaper for democratic governments than for non-democratic governments to finance the cost of building the infrastructure necessary for economic development. Secondly, easy access to credit allows democratic governments to maintain fairly stable tax rates by borrowing for unusual expenditures and spreading the cost out over many years. Such "tax smoothing" allows them to avoid drastic tax increases that would harm economic growth by creating significant market distortions.[26]

Olson is correct in emphasizing property rights as a major factor in the superior economic growth of democracies. What Olson does not say is that democracies are able to do this because democracy is *in general* a more efficient political decision-making system than dictatorship. Democracy forces leaders to adopt policies that are beneficial for society as a whole, rather than merely best for themselves. Economic growth is in the long-term interest of society as a whole, and if the government does not deliver it, voters demand new government policies more favorable to economic growth. Furthermore, voters often demand institutions like an independent judiciary or an independent central bank in order to protect property rights—and thus economic growth—from

---

[25] Schultz and Weingast (1994). Although his analysis does not differentiate countries by level of democracy, Tilly (1990) makes a similar point with regard to the Dutch Republic, the Republic of Venice, and Great Britain.

[26] Schultz and Weingast (1994).

even the voters themselves and the leaders they elect to govern them.

The superiority of democratic decision-making provides the link between the twin phenomena of democratic economic superiority and democratic peace. Without the concept of democratic efficiency, Olson's model fails to provide any apparent link between these two phenomena. As I shall illustrate in Chapter 5, it is the democratic decision-making system which limits defense spending levels. The higher the level of democratic efficiency, the fewer resources beyond legitimate defense needs are diverted from more productive investments in the economy.

Democratic Efficiency

Thus, the advantage of democracy is that democratic governments create policies that are less harmful to the economy than do non-democratic governments. In addition to providing stronger and more enduring protection of property rights, democratic governments tend to spend public funds more efficiently, while their policies entail fewer deadweight costs and create fewer economic distortions. Democracy also is the political system that most encourages innovation and human capital development, increasing total factor productivity, and thereby increasing economic growth.

In Chapter 1, I demonstrated how democracy limits corruption by public officials. I also showed how a policy-making process open to citizen input produces more efficient public policies. Bribery and the inefficient use of public funds impose deadweight costs on the economy. Those resources could be used for productive purposes that increase economic growth. Instead, they create market distortions that reduce economic growth.[27] To the extent that bribery is minimized and public funds are collected and spent in a manner that minimizes administrative costs, the economy benefits from more productive employment of capital. Democracies are superior in this regard. Furthermore, to the extent that government policies provide the most benefit for the most people possible, the economic distortions of government policies are minimized, also benefiting economic growth. Input from the citizenry makes the policies of democratic governments come closer to maximizing aggregate social welfare, thereby minimizing economic distortions and maximizing economic growth.

This openness to citizen input leaves democratic governments especially vulnerable to the effects of rent-seeking behavior by special interest groups. Democratic and non-democratic governments alike face demands upon their revenues by groups in society. Nevertheless, democracies

---

[27] One might criticize this point with regard to bribery, which is merely a transfer of resources between individuals and/or groups. In fact, it is unreasonable to expect the individuals receiving the bribes to invest 100% of their bribes, but instead, they will consume at least a portion of it. Dictators may spend the money on palaces or shoes, or even send it overseas, which in any case provides little long-term economic benefit for the economy of the dictator's country. In contrast, to the extent that competition in the market squeezes profits to the degree that economists believe, the added cost of bribery may force some firms out of business, or force them to curtail their own investments in new capital. Due to differing marginal utilities for bribe givers and takers, I expect that the net effect of this transfer of resources would be a shift of resources from investment toward consumption. This should be expected to harm long-term economic growth.

tend to mitigate the impact of such groups better than do dictatorships.

A country as a whole becomes richer through economic growth, but not everyone benefits from the innovation that leads to economic growth. The development of the mechanized tractor revolutionized agricultural production. The use of tractors made it a lot cheaper and easier to till large fields, leading to increases in farm production and lower food prices. This led to economic growth and a general increase in prosperity in countries that adopted the new technology. But the use of tractors also hurt the financial interests of those who supplied draft animals to farms.

To benefit special interests, a government can suppress innovation, but society as a whole pays the price. For example, if the horse and oxen industry had been able to convince the U.S. government to place a high enough tax on tractors and a high enough tariff on imported grain, no American farmers would have bought tractors. In the domestic market, American grain produced using draft animals would have remained competitive with imported grain produced using tractors. The draft animal industry would have remained prosperous, but American society as a whole would have forsaken cheaper food and a much higher standard of living.[28]

There will always be a constituency in favor of innovation and vested interests opposed to it. Economic growth is thus dependent not only on the availability of new inno-

---

[28] This example, of course, assumes that it is cheaper for the special interest to lobby the government than to adapt to change. I will discuss factors influencing the susceptibility of governments to special interest group pressures below.

vation, but also the extent to which a government can resist the pressure from vested interests to prevent these new innovations from taking hold. Governments constantly influence the outcomes of these struggles through legislation and regulation. They impose tariffs to prevent the importation of foreign technology or cheaper goods that will harm the vested interests of less efficient domestic competitors. They offer subsidies to encourage the use of one type of technology over another. And they build infrastructure such as roads and bridges to facilitate commerce.

The extent to which the special interests win out over the general interest with regard to innovation and economic growth depends on two factors: (1) how disproportionate (in relation to their proportion of the population) is the power of special interests in society[29] and (2) how able is the government to process (reflect upon, take into account, etc.) all of the information and pressures upon it to come up with a coherent policy. These factors together make up what I call "democratic efficiency."

Empirical Evidence

I have performed ordinary least squares regressions to examine the relationship between democratic efficiency and economic growth for sixty-eight countries worldwide.

---

[29] It is possible that a majority of the population may believe that innovation threatens their interests. In fact, this belief actually may be true in the short-term. But not in the long term. Such a myopic outlook has led to economic stagnation in several democratic countries in South Asia and Latin America. This seems, however, to indicate a learning curve, rather than undermine my argument; the public in countries as diverse as Argentina and India have elected, in the past few years, governments which have opened significantly their markets to competition and innovation.

The dependent variable is the average annual rate of change in GDP over the period 1978–92. I employ five independent variables: the initial level of development (1978 GDP per capita),[30] level of investment (average 1978–92 ratio of gross domestic investment to GDP),[31] value of human capital (average 1978–92 secondary school enrollment as a proportion of age group),[32] the distribution of power in society (Gini index of income inequality), and the degree to which interest groups are large and encompassing (Herfindahl index of labor strength and unity). Table 3 at the end of this chapter presents my results.

I make use of the first independent variable, 1978 GDP per capita, to control for economic convergence. According to neoclassical economic growth models, less developed countries should experience higher growth rates than developed countries, because the former should experience higher returns to capital than the latter. This is due to diminishing marginal returns to capital.[33] For example, consider a simple agricultural economy in which hand plows are the dominant technology. The introduction of tractors and fertilizer can greatly increase the size of harvests. An equivalent increase in yields would be difficult—if not impossible—to achieve, simply by investing the same amount of new capital in a farm that already employs capital-intensive agricultural techniques. Less developed countries can raise their economic growth rates simply through investment in more capi-

---

[30] These data come from Penn World Table 5.6.
[31] These data come from Penn World Table 5.6.
[32] These data come from the World Bank *World Development Report*.
[33] For evidence of this phenomenon, see, Barro and Sala-i-Martin (1992).

tal-intensive production techniques, that is, by emulating the techniques employed in more developed economies. But the more capital they invest, the less their economic growth rates increase, due to diminishing marginal returns.

Due to this phenomenon, one should expect, *ceteris paribus*, less developed countries to experience higher economic growth rates than developed countries. In congruence with economic theory and with the findings of Barro and Sala-i-Martin (1992), I find a slight negative relationship between a country's level of economic development and its economic growth rate. A $1,000 increase in initial GDP per capita results in a decrease in the economic growth rate of approximately 0.006 percentage points.

My second independent variable is the average amount of gross domestic investment divided by GDP. This variable indicates the amount of investment in the economy. It is a standard economic assumption that investment (increasing the amount of capital in the economy) results in economic growth. My results confirm that the investment level has a powerful impact on economic growth. A one percentage point increase in investment increases the economic growth rate by three percentage points.

As I noted above, Olson's (1993) model predicts that democracy increases investment. Interestingly, I find no significant relationship between either of the indicators of democratic efficiency and the level of investment.

My third independent variable is the average secondary school enrollment as a ratio of age group. Helliwell (1994) uses this as a measurement of human capital in his study linking human capital to the growth of per capita GDP. I find no significant relationship between this variable and overall GDP growth. I do, however, find that this measure of human capital is strongly linked to each indicator of democratic efficiency. It has a negative relationship with income inequality and a positive relationship with labor strength/unity. Apparently, although democratic efficiency is strongly linked to investment in human capital, human capital (at least as indicated by secondary school enrollments) does not impact economic growth rates.

My final two independent variables, the Gini index of income inequality and the Herfindahl index of organized labor strength and unity, are the indicators of democratic efficiency that I employ throughout Part I of this book.

The Gini index of income inequality provides an indication of the distribution of power in society. My hypothesis is that there is a negative relationship between this variable and the economic growth rate.

There is a growing literature in the field of economics indicating that an unequal distribution of wealth and/or income in society harms economic growth.[34] For example, Alberto

---

[34] See, for example, Alesina and Rodrik (1994), Galor and Zeira (1993), Perotti (1992 and 1993), and Persson and Tabellini (1991). Perotti (1993) adopts Kuznets' (1955) assumption of an inverted U-shaped relationship between income inequality and economic growth (growth initially increases inequality, but it later declines), and finds that the high inequality at the intermediate level of development causes economic growth to stall. The models of Galor and Zeira (1993) and Alesina and Rodrik (1994) do not make this assumption, but also find evidence that income inequality reduces economic growth. Rauch (1993) finds that when a country begins to industrialize, labor market distortions in urban areas often increase inequality temporarily. It would be interesting to know the extent to which this increase in inequality, and the resultant slowing of economic growth, prevents less developed countries from catching up to the standard of living of the more developed countries.

Alesina and Dani Rodrik (1994) develop a model showing that the more equally distributed is wealth in a country, the higher should be that country's economic growth rate. Like Olson, they look at the impact of taxes on economic growth rates. But their model is based on the impact of citizens' preferences for taxes (and hence redistributionary government policies). Their model assumes that the higher the proportion of one's income is derived from capital, the lower the tax rate would that individual prefer. As a result, the more equal is the distribution of capital in the economy, the more capital the median voter has. Thus, the more equal is the distribution of wealth (capital) in society, the lower will be the tax rate and the higher the growth rate. Alesina and Rodrik back up their formal model with empirical evidence showing that both an unequal distribution of wealth and an unequal distribution of income are negatively correlated with economic growth. They find that a 10% reduction in the income share of the richest 20% of the population yields a 0.33% increase in the economic growth rate.[35]

My own statistical analysis confirms their findings that there is a strong negative relationship between income inequality and GDP growth. I find that a 10% decrease in inequality results in a 0.9 percentage point increase in the GDP growth rate.

---

[35] The models presented by Galor and Zeira (1993), Perotti (1992), and Persson and Tabellini (1991) all focus on investment in human capital/education, but like Alesina and Rodrik (1994), they find that inequality reduces economic growth. Rodrik (1994) provides a case study of South Korea and Taiwan which emphasizes low inequality as a primary factor in these countries' high economic growth rates.

My final independent variable is the Herfindahl index of labor strength and unity. This variable indicates the extent to which the interests of interest groups coincide with those of society as a whole. The more these interests coincide, the less rent-seeking behavior there should be. My hypothesis is that there is a positive relationship between this variable and the GDP growth rate.

There is a wide literature concerning the role of encompassing interest groups in government policymaking and its impact on economic performance. It centers around the related concept of "democratic" or "societal" corporatism.[36] The definition of democratic corporatism (as opposed to its fascist variant) depends upon the author, but most describe it as some system under which a democratic government gives a special role to a small number of encompassing interest groups (usually labor and capital) in its decision-making processes. This role is always important in wage negotiations, but it usually extends to other policy spheres as well.

Little work directly examines the relationship between corporatism and economic growth.[37] But several

---

[36] There is a large literature devoted to the political and economic effects of corporatism. See Alvarez, et al (1991), Bruno and Sachs (1985), Calmfors and Driffill (1988), Cameron (1984), Crouch (1985), Golden, et al (1993), Headley (1970), Lange, et al (1993), Marks (1986), Schmitter (1981), Summers, et al (1993), and Wallerstein (1990).

[37] Katzenstein (1985) argues that corporatism leads to higher economic growth. Alvarez, et al (1991) argue that powerful unions are associated with lower growth rates under right-wing governments and higher growth rates under left-wing governments. Most of the corporatist literature assumes government by pro-labor (left-wing) parties, which makes these findings consistent with the overall corporatism literature.

studies have found important economic benefits from corpo-ratism, including lower inflation and lower unemployment,[38] and less distortionary taxation policies.[39] These studies imply that corporatism leads to higher economic growth rates. Low inflation coupled with low unemployment implies well-functioning markets for labor, goods, and services. This should be associated with economic growth. Furthermore, the less distortionary are taxes, the less taxation policy hinders economic activity, and this should translate into higher growth rates.

Becker's (1983 & 1985) discussion of the deadweight cost of lobbying illustrates how corporatism should benefit economic growth. If a government institutionalizes

---

[38] See Bruno and Sachs (1985), Cameron (1984), and Crouch (1985). Wallerstein (1990) explores the connection between corporatism and wage restraint by unions. Alvarez, et al (1991) argue that corporatism is associated with lower inflation only when there is a leftist government. But Marks (1986) finds a positive relationship between corporatism and the participation in government by socialist parties. This is not unexpected, since socialist parties usually claim to represent the working class, and the power of labor should be correlated with the electoral success of parties representing labor. Calmfors and Driffill (1988) argue that the relationship between corporatism and both unemployment and inflation is "hump-shaped" (the most and the least corporatist countries do the best, since at intermediate levels of power, unions are apt to attempt and succeed at rent-seeking behavior in favor of members at the expense of non-members and the rest of society).

[39] Summers, et al (1993) find that, in corporatist countries, tax rates on labor are higher and that tax rates on capital are lower. Taxes on capital are more distortionary, in general, than taxes on labor. In addition, the distortionary effects of taxes on labor in corporatist countries is lower. Unlike Alvarez, et al (1991), they find that the political orientation of the government does not affect the results.

consultation with a few peak associations, the marginal benefit of lobbying by small interest groups becomes insignificant. If lobbying costs are minimized, capital formerly consumed by the deadweight costs of lobbying can be put to more productive uses, which increases economic growth.

The finding of Summers, et al (1993) are particularly relevant to the discussion of labor power and discussion of democratic efficiency. They argue that corporatist countries are able to adopt taxation policies which impose lower deadweight costs on the economy because "encompassing unions recognize that their members bear the cost of reductions in the size of the tax base and internalize the government budget constraint in choosing wage and labor levels."[40] Unions in corporatist countries moderate their wage demands because they have to be concerned about the effects of their demands on the country's overall economic performance. This is because unions in corporatist countries are so large that their own welfare is undeniably linked with that of the economy as a whole. Furthermore, such unions accept higher taxes on their members because a tax on labor is less harmful to economic growth than a tax on capital. Once again, the size of the labor groups forces them to be concerned about overall economic growth.

The literature on corporatism seems to imply that labor power is beneficial to economic growth. But each author's rankings of corporatism differ greatly from another's, due to their subjective nature. I propose the Herfindahl index as a more objective indicator of democratic efficiency.

---

[40] Summers, et al (1993), p. 386.

Overall, I find no significant statistical relationship between the Herfindahl index and the rate of GDP growth. The absence of a relationship, however, seems to be caused by the abysmally low level of unionization in the majority of countries in my data set (and, indeed, in the majority of countries in the world). It is not entirely unexpected that very weak unions have no impact on the government policies that affect economic growth. If I eliminate those cases in which the Herfindahl index is less than 0.005 (the equivalent of only 7% of the population being unionized and represented by a single union confederation), I find a significant positive relationship between the Herfindahl index and the GDP growth rate. I find that a 10% increase in labor strength/unity increases the rate of GDP growth by approximately 0.1 percentage points.

For those countries with a Herfindahl index of less than 0.005, there is no significant relationship between the Herfindahl index and economic growth. This is not surprising, given the low level of unionization below this threshold. I expect that the Herfindahl index will become a more powerful explanatory variable in cross-national studies of less developed countries only if unionization levels in these countries rise to the point at which labor can reasonably be expected to exert real influence on government policies.

Overall, these five variables explain a great deal of the cross national variation in economic growth rates (R^2=0.38). The two indicators of democratic efficiency make a substantial contribution to this result. When I remove these two independent variables (and employ only the other three), the R^2 is only 0.15.

Conclusions

In my discussion of Olson's theory of the economic superiority of democracies, I noted that South Korea and Taiwan proved particularly problematical, since they both experienced phenomenal investment-led growth before they adopted democratic governments. Later, I presented these countries as examples of how economic development leads to democracy because human capital becomes increasingly important with development. As I developed my argument regarding democratic efficiency and the economic benefits of an equal distribution of power, these countries seemed to drop out of sight.

But not out of mind. I cannot conclude this chapter without noting Rodrik's (1994) explanation of how South Korea and Taiwan were able to achieve investment-led growth. He emphasizes that the remarkable degree of income and wealth equality in those countries helped to insulate their governments from rent-seeking behavior from interest groups. This insight demonstrates that their growth is not anomalous, but indeed entirely consistent with my theory of democratic efficiency. They grew, not despite their non-democratic governments, but *because* they exhibited a high level of democratic efficiency.

Democratic countries enjoy superior economic performance to the extent that a relatively equal distribution of power forges government policies that increase investment in human capital and raise total factor productivity. Democracy is beneficial to economic growth at all levels of economic development, and its impact on growth rates increases with a country's level of development.

Democratic efficiency provides a more precise indication of economic growth potential than merely whether or not a country is governed by democratic institutions. Both indicators of democratic efficiency demonstrate a significant impact on economic growth rates. In general, a high level of income inequality lessens economic growth and strong, unified labor organizations increase economic growth.

References

Alesina, Alberto, and Dani Rodrik. 1994. "Distributive Politics and Economic Growth." *Quarterly Journal of Economics* 109: 465–490.

Alesina, Alberto, and Lawrence H. Summers. November 1991. "Central Bank Independence and Macroeconomic Performance: Some Comparative Evidence." Unpublished manuscript.

Alvarez, Michael R., Geoffrey Garrett, and Peter Lange. 1991. "Government Partisanship, Labor Organization, and Macroeconomic Performance." *American Political Science Review* 85: 539–556.

Arat, Zehra F. 1988. "Democracy and Economic Development: Modernization Theory Revisited." *Comparative Politics* 21: 21–36.

Barro, Robert J. 1991. "Economic Growth in a Cross Section of Countries." *Quarterly Journal of Economics* 106: 407–443.

Barro, Robert J., and Xavier Sala-i-Martin. 1992. "Convergence." *Journal of Political Economy* 100: 223–251.

Becker, Gary S. 1983. "A Theory of Competition among Pressure Groups for Political Influence." *Quarterly Journal of Economics* 98: 371–700.

Becker, Gary S. 1985. "Public Policies, Pressure Groups, and Dead Weight Costs." *Journal of Public Economics* 28: 329–347.

Bhalla, Surjit. 1994. "Free Societies, Free Markets and Social Welfare." Unpublished paper presented at Nobel symposium on democracy, Uppsala University. Summarized in "Democracy and Growth," *Economist* 332: 15–17.

Bollen, Kenneth A. 1979. "Political Democracy and the Timing of Development." *American Sociological Review* 44: 572–587.

Bollen, Kenneth A. 1983. "World System Position, Dependency, and Democracy: The Cross-National Evidence." *American Sociological Review* 48: 468–79.

Bollen, Kenneth A., and Robert W. Jackman. 1985. "Political Democracy and the Size Distribution of Income." *American Sociological Review* 50: 438–457.

Brunk, Gregory G., Gregory A. Caldeira, and Michael S. Lewis-Beck. 1987. "Capitalism, Socialism, and Democracy: An Empirical Inquiry." *European Journal of Political Research* 15: 459–470.

Bruno, Michael, and Jeffrey Sachs. 1985. *The Economics of Worldwide Stagflation*. Cambridge, MA: Harvard University Press.

Burkhart, Ross E., and Michael S. Lewis-Beck. 1994. "Comparative Democracy: The Economic Development Thesis." *American Political Science Review* 88: 903–910.

Calmfors, Lars, and John Driffill. 1988. "Bargaining Structure, Corporatism, and Macroeconomic Performance." *Economic Policy* 3: 13–61.

Cameron, David R. 1984. "Social Democracy, Corporatism, Labour Quiescence and the Representation of Economic Interest in Advanced Capitalist Society." In *Order and Conflict in Contemporary Capitalism,* ed. John H. Goldthorpe. Oxford: Clarendon.

Crouch, Colin. 1985. "Conditions for Trade Union Restraint." In *The Politics of Inflation and Economic Stagnation*, ed. Leon N. Lindberg and Charles S. Maier. Washington, DC: Brookings Institution, 105–139.

Dahl, Robert. 1989. *Democracy and Its Critics*. New Haven: Yale University Press.

De Schweinitz, Karl, Jr. 1964. *Industrialization and Democracy*. New York: The Free Press of Glencoe.

Eggertsson, Thráinn. 1990. *Economic Behavior and Institutions*. Cambridge: Cambridge University Press.

Elster, Jon. 1979. *Ulysses and the Sirens*. Cambridge: Cambridge University Press.

Galor, Oded, and Joseph Zeira. 1993. "Income Distribution and Macroeconomics." *Review of Economic Studies* 60: 35–52.

Golden, Miriam, Peter Lange, and Michael Wallerstein. 1993. "Trends in Collective Bargaining and Industrial Relations in Non-Corporatist Countries." Paper delivered at Annual Meeting of the American Political Science Association.

Gonick, Lev S., and Robert M. Rosh. 1988. "The Structural Constraints of the World Economy on National Political Development." *Comparative Political Studies* 21: 171–199.

Goodman, John B. 1991. "The Politics of Central Bank Independence." *Comparative Politics* 23: 324–349.

Headley, Bruce W. 1970. "Trade Unions and National Wages Policies." *Journal of Politics* 32: 407–439.

Helliwell, John F. 1994. "Empirical Linkages Between Democracy and Economic Growth." *British Journal of Political Science* 24: 225–248.

Jackman, Robert W. 1973. "On the Relationship of Economic Development to Political Performance." *American Journal of Political Science* 17: 611–621.

Katzenstein, Peter J. 1985. *Small States in World Markets: Industrial Policy in Europe*. Ithaca, NY: Cornell University Press.

Krugman, Paul. November/December 1994. "The Myth of Asia's Miracle." *Foreign Affairs* 73: 62–78.

Kuznets, Simon. 1955. "Economic Growth and Income Inequality." *American Economic Review* 45: 1–28.

Kydland, F., and E. Prescott. 1977. "Rules Rather than Discretion: The Inconsistency of Optimal Plans." *Journal of Political Economy* 85: 473–492.

Lange, Peter, Michael Wallerstein, and Miriam Golden. 1993. "The End of Corporatism? Wage Setting in the Nordic and Germanic Countries." In Sanford Jacoby, ed., *Global Capital, Local Labor*. Oxford: Oxford University Press.

Lipset, Seymour Martin. 1959. "Some Social Requisites of Democracy." *American Political Science Review* 53: 69–105.

Lipset, Seymour Martin. 1960. *Political Man*. New York: Doubleday & Co.

Marks, Gary. 1986. "Neocorporatism and Incomes Policy in Western Europe and North America." *Comparative Politics* 18: 253–277.

North, Douglas C. 1981. *Structure and Change In Economic History*. New York: W.W. Norton & Co.

Olson, Mancur. 1982. *The Rise and Decline of Nations: Economic Growth, Stagflation, and Social Rigidities*. New Haven: Yale University Press.

Olson, Mancur. 1993. "Dictatorship, Democracy, and Development." *American Political Science Review* 87: 567–576.

Perotti, Roberto. 1992. "Income Distribution, Politics, and Growth." *American Economic Review* 82: 311–316.

Perotti, Roberto. 1993. "Political Equilibrium, Income Distribution, and Growth." *Review of Economic Studies* 60: 755–776.

Persson, Torsten and Guido Tabellini. 1991. "Is Inequality Harmful for Growth? Theory and Evidence." National Bureau of Economic Research Working Paper No. 3599.

Przeworski, Adam, and Michael Wallerstein. 1988. "Structural Dependence of the State on Capital." *American Political Science Review* 82: 11–29.

Rasmusen, Eric and J. Mark Ramseyer. 1994. "Cheap Bribes and the Corruption Ban: A Coordination Game Among Rational Legislators." *Public Choice* 78: 305–327.

Rauch, James E. 1993. "Economic Development, Urban Underemployment, and Income Inequality." *Canadian Journal of Economics* 26: 901–918.

Rodrik, Dani. 1994. "Getting Interventions Right: How South Korea and Taiwan Grew Rich." Working Paper No. 4964. National Bureau of Economic Research.

Roemer, John E. 1995. "Why the Poor Do Not Expropriate the Rich in Democracies: A New Argument." Paper presented at the UCLA Workshop in Political Economy, October 20, 1995.

Schmitter, Philippe C. 1981. "Interest Intermediation and Regime Governability." In *Organizing Interests in Western Europe: Pluralism, Corporatism, and the Transformation of Politics,* ed. Suzanne Berger, et al. Cambridge: Cambridge University Press.

Schultz, Kenneth A., and Barry R. Weingast. 1994. "The Democratic Advantage: The Institutional Sources of State Power in International Competition." Paper presented at the 1994 meeting of the American Political Science Association.

Sirowy, Larry, and Alex Inkeles. 1990. "The Effects of Democracy on Economic Growth and Inequality: A Review." *Studies in Comparative International Development* 25: 126–157.

Summers, Lawrence, Jonathan Gruber, and Rodrigo Vergara. 1993. "Taxation and the Structure of Labor Markets: The Case of Corporatism." *Quarterly Journal of Economics* 108: 385–411.

Tilly, Charles. 1990. *Coercion, Capital, and European States, A.D. 990–1990*. Oxford: Basil Blackwell.

Wallerstein, Michael. 1990. "Centralized Bargaining and Wage Restraint." *American Journal of Political Science* 34: 982–1004.

Williamson, Oliver E. 1985. *The Economic Institutions of Capitalism*. New York: The Free Press.

World Bank. 1979 edition through 1995 edition. *World Development Report*. Oxford: Oxford University Press.

Table 3

Dependent Variable
- Economic growth rate[41]

Independent Variables	*Coefficient*	*T-statistic*
• Income inequality[42]	–0.098	–2.2
• Labor strength & unity[43]	–0.014	–0.09
• Investment[44]	0.30	4.8
• Education[45]	0.0042	0.2
• Level of development[46]	0.0000058	–4.0

N=67
R^2=0.38
Adj. R^2=0.33

Unless otherwise noted, all data come from Penn World Table 5.6. GDP figures are at purchasing power parity.

[41] Average annual rate of change in GDP, 1978–1992. Calculated by author.

[42] Gini index. For formula and sources of data, see chap. 1, note 51.

[43] Herfindahl index. For formula and sources of data, see chap. 1, note 52.

[44] Gross domestic investment divided by GDP.

[45] Average secondary school enrollment rate, 1978–1992.

[46] GDP per capita, 1978.

Dependent Variable
- Economic growth rate

Independent Variables	*Coefficient*	*T-statistic*
• Investment	15.1	2.6
• Education	0.56	0.3
• Level of development	−0.00042	−4.0

N=112
R^2=0.15
Adj. R^2=0.13

Dependent Variable
- Economic growth rate

Independent Variables	*Coefficient*	*T-statistic*
• Income inequality	0.084	1.0
• Labor strength & unity	0.26	2.7
• Investment	0.20	2.2
• Education	−0.0087	−0.3
• Level of development	0.0000014	−1.0

N=20 (Countries with Hefindahl index > 0.005)
R^2=0.46
Adj. R^2=0.27

4

Trade Protectionism

Trade, economists argue, occurs naturally. Economists employ the Heckscher-Ohlin model of international trade to demonstrate that trade is a positive sum game between countries, and that the nature of goods traded is a function of the trading partners' comparative advantages.[1]

The fact that trade should occur, however, says nothing about the amount of trade to expect. Indeed, imports and exports as a share of GDP vary considerably cross-nationally. For example the value of exports and imports as a percentage of GDP range from a mere 18% for India to 343% for Singapore.[2]

---

[1] For a basic introduction to international trade theory, see Krugman and Obstfeld (1991) and Salvatore (1990). For a more sophisticated discussion, see Baldwin (1984) or Dixit and Norman (1980).
[2] The data come from the Penn World Table 5.6.

Part of this variation can be explained simply by the size of the country. India is one of the most populous countries in the world. Singapore is a tiny city-state. The smaller a country is, the harder it is for it to produce domestically all of the inputs necessary for production and all of the goods that consumers may wish to purchase. In essence, a large country can achieve economies of scale in large numbers of industries more easily than a small country.

But country size accounts for only part of such variation. Indeed, governments employ a variety of methods to protect domestic industries from foreign competition. For example, virtually all countries impose tariffs on various imported goods. In addition, governments employ a variety of nontariff barriers, such as subsidies to domestic industries, quotas on foreign imports, and even excessive red-tape for foreign exporters.[3]

Trade barriers are quite costly—not only to the country whose exports are restricted, but also to the country which restricts them. For example, the World Bank estimates that quantitative restrictions on textiles, automobiles, and steel cost the U.S. economy $13.06 billion, $6.9 billion, and $910 million, respectively, in 1985.[4] Similarly, the U.S. International Trade Commission estimated that restrictions on Japanese automobile exports to the U.S., 1981–84, saved 44,000 jobs in the U.S. automobile industry at a cost of $100,000 each (nearly three times the annual salary of an

---

[3] For example, France once required that all VCRs be inspected by one small customs office before entering the country, rather than allowing them to be inspected at any customs office. This creative nontariff barrier greatly restricted French imports of Japanese VCRs.

[4] Salvatore (1990), p. 263.

autoworker). The total cost to American consumers, in terms of higher automobile prices, was $15.7 billion.[5]

Trade protectionism is an ideal subject for democratic efficiency analysis. Since free trade is the policy that normally maximizes income for the economy as a whole, protectionism is employed specifically to benefit special interests. For example, quotas on sugar imports into the U.S. raise sugar prices only a few dollars per person annually, but generate $600 million in rents for a few thousand American sugar producers.[6] A country's level of democratic efficiency indicates the extent to which power is distributed equally. The more unequally power is distributed, the greater the ability of special interests to use their disproportionate power to shape trade policies to benefit them, regardless of the cost to society as a whole. The lower a country's level of democratic efficiency, the more rent-seeking behavior should exist in the arena of trade policy, and thus, the more protectionist should trade policy be. If we control for country size, then democratic efficiency should be positively related to the amount of trade that a given country engages in.

Review of the literature

Economists have a lot to say about the effect of trade policy on the distribution of income. Unfortunately, they have little to say about the inverse of this relationship. But even to the extent that they examine the impact of trade protectionism on the income distribution, most work centers on the relative gains/losses of classes (labor, capitalists, and

---

[5] Salvatore (1990), p. 255.
[6] Salvatore (1990), p. 262.

landowners), rather than on the overall income distribution in society. Most of this literature stems from the Stolper-Samuelson theorem. This theorem states that a tariff benefits the owners of the factor of production (land, labor, or capital) that is scarce domestically in relation to the protectionist country's trading partner. For example, the Heckscher-Ohlin model indicates that if labor is scarce in Country A relative to country B, then Country A should import labor-intensive goods. The Stolper-Samuelson theorem points out that labor in Country A should favor protection, because it would increase the demand for labor and thereby raise wages. The same bias toward protectionism occurs on the part of land or capital in cases where either of those factors is relatively scarce. The windfall enjoyed by the scarce factor is at the expense of the abundant factors, and overall, the country is poorer as a result of the protection.[7]

Rogowski (1989) presents bountiful cross-national evidence that the backers of protection are usually the owners of the scarce factors of production. The relative abundance or scarcity of a factor of production, however, says nothing about the number of individuals in each category,

---

[7] Metzler (1949) points out that this result occurs only when world demand for a country's exports is elastic. If world demand is inelastic, the results will be reversed: the tariff will increase the income of the abundant factor, decrease the income of the scarce factor, and increase income overall. Cases of inelastic world demand, however, are very rare and tend to be short-lived. For example, before the first oil shock, world demand for oil from OPEC was fairly inelastic, due to its near monopoly on the supply of oil in world markets. In fact, the increase in price resulted in substitutes being found; more intensive oil exploration, conservation, and the emergence of non-OPEC oil exporters, such as Mexico and Norway, dampened world demand for OPEC oil.

and therefore, says little about the overall distribution of income in society. Labor in Country A might be scarce, relative to Country B, while the number of workers in Country A greatly outnumber landowners and capitalists. How, then, does a tariff affect the distribution of income? This question cannot be answered without detailed knowledge of the degree to which ownership of capital and land (wealth) is concentrated. Employing the distribution of income as an independent (rather than dependent) variable eliminates this problem.

By the same token, if labor successfully demands protection, does this mean that power is more equally distributed than in cases where it is unsuccessful? Or does it mean that certain segments of the labor movement were able to demand protection for their industries, while others were not?

Several recent studies, in fact, relax the assumption that labor is a monolithic interest group.[8] Adrian Wood (1994), for example, argues that increased trade between developed countries (DCs) and less developed countries (LDCs) in recent years has increased income inequality in the former and decreased it in the latter. This is because the LDCs have relatively more low-skilled labor and the DCs have relatively more highly-skilled labor. Increased trade has resulted in the specialization of LDCs in the export of goods manufactured by low-skilled workers, while DCs have specialized in goods manufactured by highly-skilled workers. This has increased the demand for low-skilled workers in LDCs and decreased such demand in DCs. The wages of low-skilled

---

[8] See Burtless (1995) for a good review of the literature.

workers in LDCs thus have risen relative to those of highly-skilled workers, thereby decreasing income inequality. The reverse has occurred in DCs.

This analysis comes closer to explaining the impact of trade policy on the distribution of income than studies that treat workers as a monolithic interest group. It indicates that free trade can affect the gross distribution of income (before taxes and government transfers). This figure, however, is unlikely to prove a very accurate measure of the distribution of power in society. It is the *net* distribution of income that reflects the actual resources that individuals command. This figure more accurately reflects the distribution of power in society than the gross distribution of income.

While various economists point out circumstances in which protection benefits certain segments of society, they nearly universally agree that free trade maximizes the overall income of a country. To the extent that the elimination of trade barriers harms certain segments of society or certain economic sectors (depending on which of the above analyses you prefer), aggregate social welfare is maximized by a policy of free trade coupled with a re-distribution of some of the benefits from "winners" to "losers."[9] The increase in income overall is large enough to make sure that everyone benefits. The real question is whether the political markets are efficient enough to allow the economic markets to function optimally.

---

[9] Dixit and Norman (1980) demonstrate that free trade is always the welfare maximizing policy and that "losers" can be compensated for any losses they incur from the elimination of trade barriers, thereby counteracting any adverse effects that the elimination of trade barriers might have on the distribution of income in society.

Here is where democratic efficiency is analytically useful. Free trade maximizes aggregate social welfare. From a political standpoint, however, free trade is the optimal policy only to the extent that it benefits powerful interests to a degree commensurate with their power. The more equally power is distributed, the more equally the benefits of trade policy must be distributed. The more unequally power is distributed, the more disproportionately the benefits of trade must be distributed to the more powerful groups in society. Regardless of the size of the economic "pie," it is not hard to insure that benefits accrue to a small elite. But the more widely the benefits must be distributed, the more difficult it is to distribute those benefits to one interest group without taking them away from another. The solution to this dilemma is to increase the size of the "pie." Free trade increases the size of the pie.

The degree of trade protectionism should be inversely related to a country's level of democratic efficiency. The more equally power is distributed, the more widely the benefits of trade policy must be distributed, and therefore, the stronger the imperative for the government to follow a policy of free trade.

Research Design

It is difficult to measure directly the level of trade protectionism in a way that is comparable cross-nationally. One choice would be to look at average tariff rates. This presents several problems. First of all, this method overemphasizes the tariffs on goods imported in small amounts and underemphasizes the tariffs on goods imported in large amounts. This is the effect of averaging the tariff rates. To a large extent, this problem can be overcome by substituting data on effective tariff rates[10] for nominal tariff rates, but effective tariff rates have to be calculated on a good by good basis, and therefore data are unavailable for most imports in most countries. Even if such data were available, however, they would not give a very accurate picture of comparative levels of trade protectionism.

This is because, as tariff rates have been steadily declining worldwide since the end of World War II, nontariff barriers have become increasingly significant. Average tariff rates (whether nominal or effective) do not take into account this increasingly important aspect of trade protectionism.

One can take into account the impact of both tariff and nontariff barriers by examining a country's total volume of trade. A country's exports and imports as a percentage of GDP should be inversely related to the magnitude of its tariff and nontariff barriers. Such data can be used for cross-national comparisons as long as one controls for the impact of country size.[11]

My dependent variable is the total value of exports and imports as a percentage of GDP.[12] My independent variables are the Gini index of income inequality, the Herfindahl

---

[10] The effective rate of protection weights each tariff according to their impact on the economy, which is accomplished by calculations based on the value added of the good subject to tariff. See Krugman and Obstfeld (1991), pp. 186–187 and Salvatore (1990), pp. 214–219.

[11] As I stated above, the smaller a country, the less self-sufficient it can be, due to difficulties in gaining economies of scale, and therefore, the greater its volume of trade must necessarily be. In general, the natural log of a country's population tends to have an inverse linear relationship with the volume of trade.

[12] The data come from the Penn World Table 5.6.

index of labor strength and unity, and the natural log of population. The latter variable controls for the impact of population size on the degree to which a country trades.[13]

I examine the relationship between these variables by means of ordinary least squares regression.

Empirical Evidence

As Table 4 indicates, there is a significant negative relationship between a country's level of income inequality and the volume of its trade. A 10 percentage point increase in income inequality results in a 16 percentage point decline in trade. There is not a significant relationship, however, between labor power and the volume of trade. Perhaps this is because labor is too divided and weak in most countries for it to have a significant effect upon trade policy.

Conclusions

Overall, the evidence lends qualified support to my hypothesis that a country's level of trade protectionism is inversely related to its level of democratic efficiency.

---

[13] See p. 106.

References

Baldwin, Robert E. 1984. "Trade Policy in Developed Countries." In *Handbook of International Economics,* ed. Ronald W. Jones and Peter B. Kenen. Amsterdam: North-Holland.

Burtless, Gary. 1995. "International Trade and the Rise in Earnings Inequality." *Journal of Economic Literature* 33: 800–816.

Dixit, Avinash, and Victor Norman. 1980. *Theory of International Trade*. Cambridge: Cambridge University Press.

Krugman, Paul R., and Maurice Obstfeld. 1991. *International Economics: Theory and Practice*. Second Edition. New York: Harper Collins.

Metzler, Lloyd A. 1949. "Tariffs, the Terms of Trade, and the Distribution of National Income." *Journal of Political Economy* 57: 1–29.

Rogowski, Ronald. 1989. *Commerce and Coalitions: How Trade Affects Domestic Political Alignments*. Princeton, NJ: Princeton University Press.

Salvatore, Dominick. 1990. *International Economics*. Third Edition. New York: Macmillan.

Wood, Adrian. 1994. *North–South Trade, Employment and Inequality: Changing Fortunes in a Skill-Driven World.* Oxford: Clarendon Press.

Table 4

Dependent Variable
- Openness to international trade[14]

Independent Variables	*Coefficient*	*T-statistic*
• Income inequality[15]	–159	–2.2
• Labor strength & unity[16]	–293	–1.3
• Country size[17]	–18	–4.4

N=57
R^2=0.28
Adj. R^2=0.24

---

[14] Sum of exports and imports as a percentage of GDP, 1988.

[15] Gini index. For formula and sources of data, see chap. 1, note 51.

[16] Herfindahl index. For formula and sources of data, see chap. 1, note 52.

[17] Natural log of 1988 population.

5

Defense Spending

Defense spending ... is unproductive for all and unavoidable for most. Rather than increased well-being, their reward is in the maintenance of their autonomy.

—Kenneth N. Waltz[1]

The world can be a dangerous place for nation-states. One scholar calculated that there had been a war, on average, every 0.4 years between 1648 and 1964.[2] To protect themselves against external threats, even the most peace-loving governments are forced to spend scarce resources on military power. Military spending levels, however, vary widely from one country to the next. In 1992, for example, military spending as a fraction of GDP ranged from 0.4% (Mauritius)

---

[1] Waltz (1979), p. 107.
[2] Wright (1965), tables 34–42 and Appendix C.

to 62.4% (Kuwait).[3] Many factors help to explain such variation. In this case, one may remark that Mauritius is an isolated island far from hostile neighbors, whereas Kuwait had recently regained its independence after having been forcibly occupied by a hostile neighboring country. It is often more difficult, however, to explain why countries in the same geographic region have greatly differing levels of military spending. This chapter will examine how democratic efficiency can help to explain such variations.

One can expect, like Waltz, that governments will try to spend as little as possible on defense. Indeed, numerous studies have found that there is a trade-off between military spending and economic growth, generally attributable to a resultant decrease in private sector investment.[4] These studies imply that, the more a government spends on its military right now, the less it will have to spend in the future. But even if one is skeptical of the literature claiming that defense spending tends to reduce economic growth, one must admit that governments will face some kind of guns/butter tradeoff as long as they have limited resources. Defense spending, like every other use of national resources, entails a certain

---

[3] International Institute for Strategic Studies (1993–94), pp. 224–228.

[4] There exists a voluminous literature from both sides of the Atlantic on this subject. See, for example, Cappelen, et al (1984); Chan (1985); DeGrasse (1983); Dumas (1986); Lindgren (1984); Mintz and Huang (1990); Ogden (1988); Reppy (1985); Smith (1980); and Thompson and Zuk (1980). Mintz and Stevenson (1992) find no relationship between military spending and short-term economic growth. They admit, however, that their study does not indicate whether or not military spending harms long-term economic growth, or whether it lessens growth indirectly—such as through crowding out investment, as is suggested by Smith (1980).

opportunity cost. Every dollar spent on the military could have been spent on anything from health care to subsidies for farmers.

On the other hand, as Waltz correctly points out, governments can do none of these things if they are overthrown by invading armies. The vast majority of citizens should be expected to favor at least the level of defense spending necessary to deter and/or repel attacks by foreign powers. A rational government should determine how much defense spending is necessary based on an objective calculation of the foreign military threats that it faces.

Realism

A popular theory of international relations called "realism"[5] looks at the problem of defense spending from this perspective. This theory claims that the foreign policy of every country is determined by its irresistible impulse to attempt to maximize its power in relation to that of its neighbors. Moreover, realism asserts that the international behavior of states is determined solely by considerations of power relative to other states in the international system. Governments gauge threats based on foreign countries' objective offensive capabilities, rather than on anything institutional, sociological, or ideological. Therefore, states of similar size located in the same geographic region should face similar levels of external threat and have similar levels of military spending. To the extent that some countries in a given region have higher

---

[5] The two pre-eminent post-war theorists of realism are Hans J. Morgenthau and Kenneth N. Waltz. See, for example Morgenthau (1973), Waltz (1979).

or lower levels of military spending, these differences should be based on objective international strategic criteria, rather than on social, ideological, or domestic political factors.[6]

Thus, taken to its logical conclusion, realism predicts spiraling arms races. If Country X arms itself to defend itself against the military capabilities of its neighbors, each of its neighbors will in turn feel threatened by Country X's arms build-up and will feel compelled to respond in kind. Their own arms build-ups make each of their neighbors—including Country X—feel less secure, and will compel each of them to buy more arms. If one takes this "security dilemma"[7] to its logical conclusion, a government should spend more and more money on its military until its own economy—or those of its rivals—collapses. While this may have occurred in a few isolated cases (such as that of 17th century Spain, or more recently, the U.S.S.R.), it is far from the norm.

---

[6] There is a large literature devoted to the subject of arms races and the determinants of military spending. Perhaps the work most influential in the development of this literature is Richardson (1960). Richardson creates a model which assumes that, for any two countries, the military spending of each should increase proportionately to that of the other country, decrease proportionately to the economic burden of military spending (see note 4, above, for a discussion of this relationship), and increase based on its level of grievances with the other country. Simaan and Cruz (1975) use formal theory to explore the implications of Richardson's model, while Brams, et al (1979) employ a game theoretic approach to the superpower arms race. Brito and Intriligator (1985) develop a formal model that takes into account imperfect information on either side and the option of payoffs by one side to the other to avoid war. Powell's (1993) formal model specifically addresses the choice between economic and military spending, while operationalizing the security dilemma and the shadow of the future.

[7] This term was coined by Herz (1950), p. 157.

Many cases contradict realist assumptions. For example, Canada and Mexico should be spending enormous sums of money on defense in efforts to deter attack by the United States. On the contrary, these two countries have among the lowest levels of defense spending in the world. Military forces do not patrol their borders with the U.S. to defend against possible attack; indeed, these mutual borders are two of the longest undefended international borders in the world.[8] To remark that Canada and Mexico both have excellent relations with the U.S. only highlights the problems with realist expectations: if a country's foreign policy is formulated solely in reaction to the offensive military capabilities of its neighbors, mutual suspicion and arms races should be the rule between neighboring countries. Clearly this is not the case in North America.

Realism does not assume that countries spend money on their militaries merely to deter and/or repel attack by their

---

[8] A realists might try to argue that the United States views its neighbors as buffer states or satellite states. It is very difficult, however, to make this case. "Buffer" against whom? No American rival lies to the south of Mexico. Thousands of miles of polar ice cap separated Canada and the former U.S.S.R., while the U.S. and U.S.S.R. were separated by only about a mile in the Bering Straits. Furthermore, it is difficult to depict either Canada or Mexico as a satellite of the U.S. Mexico's foreign and economic policies have long been at odds with those of the U.S. This has only changed since the late 1980s. Although Canada's policies have tended to be more in sync with those of the U.S., the Canadian government is democratically elected. The CIA has been accused of meddling in the political systems of many countries, but never (to my knowledge) Canada. Finally, it has been nearly a century since an American government even contemplated the possibility of employing military force against either of its neighbors.

neighbors; it claims that they also attempt to manipulate the balance of power in their favor. Military power should be employed to pressure one's neighbors to do what one wants them to do—either directly (war) or indirectly (coercion). In the words of Carl von Clausewitz so often cited by realists, "war is the mere continuation of policy by other means ... a real political instrument ... a continuation of political commerce."[9]

Thus, the other side of the North American paradox is equally paradoxical. Why hasn't the United States used its military superiority to annex Canada and/or Mexico? Both countries are temptingly endowed with rich natural resources and neither has much capability to resist a U.S. attack. But the U.S. instead prefers to pursue free trade agreements with these countries.

Japan presents another puzzle. Japan possesses the second largest GDP in the world and is one of the most technologically-advanced nations as well. It has within its grasp the means to be a superpower. It could use its wealth and technology to create a military capable of dominating Asia and challenging American hegemony around the globe. But since the restoration of Japanese sovereignty after the American occupation, and despite repeated American pleas to increase its military spending, the Japanese government has tried to limit military spending to no more than 1% of GDP (the U.S. spends about 3%).[10] Japan, rather than trying to maximize its power through military expansion, has

---

[9] Clausewitz (1976), chapter 1, part 24.

[10] This figure is for 1999. See Stockholm International Peace Research Institute (2001). As recently as 1985, the U.S. spent 6.9% of its GDP on defense.

severely limited its military spending. Rather than building a nuclear deterrent against its traditional adversaries, Russia and China (nuclear-armed since the 1950s and 1960s), Japan instead has relied upon the nuclear umbrella of another former adversary, the United States.

The member states of the European Union present another puzzle. Arguably, these states have maintained the most intense rivalries in the history of international relations. They have fought dozens of the bloodiest wars in human history, including both World Wars. Their international behavior provided the model for realism. But today, rather than threatening each other with military might, they are dismantling their common borders and moving ever closer to federalism.

Democracy seems to transcend the security dilemma. Democratic countries often do not seem to feel threatened by the military spending of their democratic neighbors. In fact, democracy seems to do more than transcend the security dilemma—it reverses it. In many cases, democratic countries feel *more* secure when their democratic neighbors increase their own defense spending. During the past couple of decades, the issue of "burden-sharing" has been one of the major sources of tension between the U.S. and both its NATO allies and Japan. The U.S. government has consistently pressured the Europeans and Japanese to spend *more* on defense, despite the fact that the rising economic power of the European Union and Japan increasingly has challenged American hegemony. It seems that, despite its effect on the relative power of states, greater military spending by one democracy *enhances* (rather than threatens) the security of another.

Incorrect fundamental assumptions may be to blame for these many cases which seem to contradict the expectations of realism. Realism claims that countries base their defense policies solely upon the military balance of power. There are, of course, dozens of ways that domestic politics may intrude upon defense policy decision-making. For example, a government may purchase weapons because arms manufacturers are politically influential, because legislators have financial interests in arms contracting firms, or even because the government relies on the military to remain in power. Realism rejects the possibility that, in equilibrium, domestic political or social factors affect defense policy.[11] If one can show a consistent pattern of such factors having a significant impact upon defense spending levels, then this fundamental assumption of realism is incorrect.

One must admit that realists are correct to the extent that some minimal level of defense spending is necessary, based on an objective evaluation of foreign threats. Such defense spending is like fire insurance: the insured pays lots of money and receives nothing in return until disaster strikes. If we extend this analogy a bit, one should expect that some governments will be more risk-averse than others, and that such governments may wish to purchase higher levels of insurance (defense) than their neighbors. Differing levels of risk aversion alone, however, would not explain a relationship between military spending and income inequality or la-

---

[11] Realists might similarly argue that countries must structure their political systems such that decisions regarding levels of military spending are insulated from the pressures of domestic politics, and that countries which do not do so get eliminated in war. The result of such Darwinian natural selection is that the surviving states are those which base their defense policies solely on the military balance of power. The end result is the same.

bor power. But rent-seeking behavior by domestic interest groups would explain this.

Interest Groups and Military Spending

Like any other government expenditure, defense spending benefits some groups in society disproportionately. Everyone benefits from the public good that is national defense, but soldiers and military contractors benefit more than other citizens. Sometimes, politicians also benefit disproportionately (financially or politically). Often, in societies characterized by great inequality, high military spending is necessary to prevent the revolt of the masses against the privileged few. For example, Machiavelli (1965) argues that non-democratic regimes can remain in power by repressive means only in countries characterized by great inequality; if the level of equality is too high, the cost of such repression becomes prohibitive, making democratic government more cost-effective.

It does not really matter who benefits disproportionately from military spending; the point is that some group always does. The cost, however, is generally spread widely throughout society (in the form of taxes). Small groups tend to have superior organizational power for collective action[12] and tend to be successful in extracting subsidies or "rents" from society. This is because the dispersed cost of such rents provides low incentives for strenuous opposition.[13] Thus, the interest groups favoring military spending in excess of what is necessary for legitimate defense needs should be expected to achieve some degree of success.

---

[12] Olson (1965).

[13] Olson (1982).

Democratic efficiency measures the equality by which power to influence government policy is distributed in a society. The higher the level of democratic efficiency in a given society, the less able are special interests in that society to extract rents from the government at the expense of the general welfare. Thus, the higher the level of democratic efficiency, the less "excess" money should the government be expected to spend on the military, beyond what is necessary based on objective strategic criteria.

Many scholars have claimed that there is a connection between military spending and social inequality.[14] They claim that the rich and privileged historically have used the military to maintain their privileged positions in society, either directly, through repression, or indirectly, by fostering nationalism through engaging in wars to distract the public from social problems.

My measurements of democratic efficiency, income distribution and the power of the labor movement, indicate the level of social inequality. Income distribution is used as a proxy for the distribution of wealth. As I outlined in Chapter 1, wealth tends to bring political influence in capitalist societies. The more unequally wealth is distributed, the more unequally political power also tends to be distributed. This unequal distribution of power empowers various groups to extract rents from the government. The "logic of collective action" gives an advantage to the small group benefiting from excessive military spending over the rest of society,

---

[14] Veblen (1939), Schumpeter (1951), and Moore (1966), for example, all claim that 19th and 20th century German belligerence was the legacy of social inequality or of traditionally privileged groups acting to maintain their traditional privileges.

which bears the cost. Thus, a given country may be prone to "excessive" military spending simply because some group in society benefits disproportionately from military spending and has the political clout to demand high defense budgets.

A weak labor movement also indicates an unequal distribution of power. As I showed in Chapter 1, a united labor movement facilitates the transmission of the preferences of workers (and by parallel, others) to the government and results in more efficient government decision-making. While defense industry labor unions may favor high military spending, unions in other industries should not share this preference, because their members do not reap disproportionate benefits from it (and may be harmed from it to the extent that military spending diverts investment from other industries). Defense industry unions do not generally dominate the labor movement. Therefore, to the extent that organized labor forms a united front in its efforts to influence government policy, labor's incentive should be to try to minimize excess military spending (which is paid for by members' taxes).[15] The larger the percentage of the population that is represented by the labor confederation, the more the preferences of the membership will reflect the preferences of the society as a whole. Thus, the more encompassing and centralized is the labor movement, the more willing and able it will be to

---

[15] As I indicated above, even if military spending is seen as a way to spur a sluggish economy or to provide jobs, there are more efficient ways of meeting these goals. The government can instead, for example, increase spending on health or education. In the short-term such spending would provide at least as much economic stimulus and at least as many jobs as increased military spending; in the long term it would provide greater benefits than military spending by raising the value of human capital.

counteract the pressure of special interest groups lobbying for rents, including excess military spending.

What is Excessive Military Spending?

How can one determine whether a country's military spending is excessive? To determine the level of threat, even realists agree that a government should examine how much its neighbors spend on their militaries. But should a country be expected to try to match the sum of all the defense spending of all of its neighbors? This might be necessary if it hoped to deter attack by all of its neighbors at once. But such a policy is, of course, untenable, if followed by one's neighbors as well. If the logic of this "super security dilemma" holds, defense budgets would increase exponentially until the economies of all involved collapsed. Since this has never occurred, one must surmise that countries judge their defense needs by some other standard.

Another possibility might be that countries try to spend as much as their highest-spending neighbor. This, however, leaves countries with small economies unable to compete with their neighbors with large economies. If Country A has a GDP one-third the size of that of Country B, Country A must spend three times the fraction of its GDP on defense as does Country B. The result of such policies would be that the economies of small countries would collapse from the strain of such competition, or that small countries would be swallowed up by larger countries.

Darwinian natural selection, however, does not seem to extend very well to the field of international relations. Although scores of European countries disappeared during the 19th century, due to the Napoleonic wars and Italian and German unification, many new countries were born at the same time in Central and South America. Any trend toward fewer countries, however, has undergone a strong and unmistakable reversal during the 20th century. For example, the collapse of the Austro-Hungarian and Ottoman empires created dozens of new countries after World War I. During the 1950s and 1960s the European colonial powers relinquished most of their colonies, creating scores more new countries in Asia and Africa. More recently, the Soviet Union has splintered into fifteen separate countries. Countries seem to be much more likely, in general, to "appear" than to "disappear," and the average country size has been decreasing for generations.

Another possibility is to assume that governments behave like other consumers of insurance: the amount that they purchase depends to a great extent on the opportunity cost. Governments are under constant pressure to provide subsidies and services beyond their fiscal abilities. In general, government revenues are limited by the size of the economy. The burden that defense places on an economy is most accurately measured by the percentage of national income that must be spent on it. Indeed, as noted above, the Japanese government purposely limits its defense spending to 1% of GDP. While most other governments do not abide by such explicit limits, the fact remains that the economic burden of defense spending is often a weighty consideration.

Thus, a country can be said to engage in "excessive" military spending if it spends a significantly higher percentage of its GDP on the military than do its neighbors.

Empirical Evidence

I hypothesize that comparative levels of military spending within a given geographic region are correlated with comparative levels of democratic efficiency. I examine this relationship by performing ordinary least squares regressions. My dependent variable is military spending as a percentage of GDP[16] and my independent variables are a Gini index of income inequality and a Herfindahl index of labor movement strength and centralization.

I must caution the reader that my results are preliminary and that I claim merely that they are consistent with, rather than definitively prove, the theoretical argument that forms the basis of this study.

The explanatory power of these results is limited by the relatively low number of cases for which data were available. First of all, I excluded Communist countries, because labor unions there in most cases were controlled by the government, and because income distribution is not an adequate indicator of the distribution of power in non-market economies. This ruled out Eastern Europe. Data were not widely available on income distribution in most African and non-Communist Asian countries. As a result, I selected the regions of Western Europe, Central America/Caribbean, and South America.

I grouped countries by geographic region, assuming that policymakers base their spending decisions on the spending patterns of neighboring countries. It is more logical to compare the military spending levels of Guatemala

---

[16] The data come from International Institute for Strategic Studies and from Stockholm International Peace Research Institute.

and Honduras, for instance, than those of Guatemala and Germany. This assumption, coupled with the limited availability of income data from developing countries, left relatively low numbers of cases from Latin America. But there were a larger number of cases from Europe.

My data sets each covered a five-year period. I made use of the average military spending for the entire period for each country. Since military spending fluctuates greatly from one year to the next for many countries, this averaging helped to protect my results from being overly influenced by a year of unusually high or low military spending. I chose a particular set of five consecutive years based upon the availability of data on income inequality. For many countries, there were gaps of ten or even twenty years between samples. I chose a given set of years for a particular region because those were the years in which income distribution studies were conducted in the greatest number of countries.

Table 5 provides support for my hypothesis of a negative relationship between democratic efficiency and comparative military spending levels. In general, income inequality tends to bear a fairly strong positive relationship with comparative military spending levels in all regions; labor power bears a negative relationship with comparative military spending levels in Latin America, but is insignificant in Europe. In the case of South America, for example, a 10 percentage point increase in income inequality results in a 1.1 percentage point increase in military spending/GDP. Similarly, a 10 percentage point increase in labor strength and unity results in a 10 percentage point decrease in military spending/GDP.

The R^2 for the multivariate regressions ranged from a low of 0.51 (Europe) to a high of 0.92 (South America).

The t-statistic for the Gini index fell below 3 only in the case of Central America. This, however, may be a function of the low degrees of freedom, due to the low number of cases. When the Gini index is used as the sole independent variable for Central America, the t-statistic rises to 3.1.

The Herfindahl index was extremely significant for the South American data set. Admittedly, the t-statistic of –6.5 was largely due to the fact that high labor power in Brazil compensates for high income inequality in reference to low military spending.

Although the Herfindahl t-statistic was low for Central America in the multivariate regression, when I omitted the Gini index as an independent variable, the t-statistic became a more respectable –2.3. This problem, again, may simply be caused by the low number of cases available.

The Herfindahl index was not significant for the European cases. This may be due to the fact that several European countries have large arms industries and are major arms exporters, a fact which may make unions more favorably disposed toward spending tax dollars on arms. Furthermore, Sweden was an outlier. This is probably due to historical/cultural reasons. Although Sweden currently has the strongest and most united labor movement in Europe, for the past century it has successfully avoided the wars that plagued Europe by pursuing a policy of armed neutrality (which necessitates relatively high defense budgets).

Conclusions

This chapter explores the relationship between democratic efficiency and military spending. I propose that democratic efficiency indicates the power of rent-seeking interest groups in society. The higher the level of democratic efficiency, the better able is the government to resist the pressures of such groups, including those seeking unnecessarily high levels of military spending. Differences in two measures of democratic efficiency—income inequality and labor power—help to explain differences in military spending levels in several geographic regions. In general, the more equally power is distributed in the society, and the more efficiently social preferences are conveyed to the government, the less a given country spends on its military in relation to its neighbors. The higher the level of democratic efficiency in a given society, the better able are citizens to demand that government spend no more money than necessary for defense, and the better able are they to counteract the rent-seeking behavior of militarist special interest groups.

These findings contradict the realist assumption that international considerations alone determine the foreign policy of states. Military spending—the major determinant of military power—is sensitive to a country's social structure. High military spending is not solely the result of threatening neighbors or some expansionist imperative in international relations; it can be merely the by-product of social inequality.

These results may also help to explain why democratic countries tend not to go to war with one another. Countries with high levels of democratic efficiency tend to spend less money on their militaries than do their neighbors. Excess military spending should contribute to the insecurity of neighboring countries, and therefore countries with high levels of democratic efficiency should be less responsible for arms races than states characterized by low levels of democratic efficiency. This may make democratically-efficient countries appear less threatening to one another, facilitating alliances with one another. Democracies, in general, have high levels of democratic efficiency and tend to be geographically clustered, making alliances desirable. If neighboring countries become allies, neither ally needs to be overly concerned about defending against the other, and each can reap the economic benefits of further reducing its military spending levels. This is certainly a subject that warrants further research.

References

Brams, Steven J., Morton D. Davis, and Philip D. Straffin, Jr. 1979. "The Geometry of the Arms Race." *International Studies Quarterly* 23: 567–598.

Brito, Dagobert L., and Michael D. Intriligator. 1985. "Conflict, War, and Redistribution." *American Political Science Review* 79: 943–957.

Cappelen, Adne, Nils Petter Gleditsch, and Olav Bjerkholt. 1984. "Military Spending and Economic Growth in the OECD Countries." *Journal of Peace Research* 21: 360–373.

Chan, Steve. 1985. "The Impact of Defense Spending on Economic Performance: A Survey of Evidence and Problems." *Orbis* 29: 403–434.

Clausewitz, Carl von. 1976. *On War*. Princeton: Princeton University Press.

DeGrasse, Robert W. Jr. 1983. *Military Expansion, Economic Decline*. New York: Council on Economic Priorities.

Dixon, Wilfred J., and Frank J. Massey, Jr. 1957. *Introduction to Statistical Analysis* (2nd Edition). New York: McGraw-Hill.

Dumas, Lloyd J. 1986. "The Military Burden on the Economy." *Bulletin of the Atomic Scientists* 42: 22–32.

Herz, John H. 1950. "Idealist Internationalism and the Security Dilemma." *World Politics* 2.

International Institute for Strategic Studies. Various years. *The Military Balance*. London: Brassey's.

Lindgren, Goran. 1984. "Armaments and Economic Performance in Industrialized Market Economies," *Journal of Peace Research* 21: 375–387.

Machiavelli, Niccolo. 1965. "A Discourse on Remodeling the Government of Florence." In *Machiavelli: The Chief Works and Others*, vol. I, trans. Allan Gilbert. Durham, NC: Duke University Press, 101–115.

Mintz, Alex, and Chi Huang. 1990. "Defense Expenditures, Economic Growth, and the 'Peace Dividend.'" *American Political Science Review* 84: 1283–1293.

Mintz, Alex and Randolph Stevenson. December 1992. "Defense Expenditures, Economic Growth, and the 'Peace Dividend': A Longitudinal Analysis of 103 Countries." Unpublished manuscript.

Moore, Barrington, Jr. 1966. *Social Origins of Dictatorship and Democracy: Lord and Peasant in the Making of the Modern World*. Boston: Beacon Press.

Morgenthau, Hans. 1973. *Politics Among Nations*. New York: Knopf.

Ogden, Michael Dee. 1988. "Military Spending Erodes Real National Security." *Bulletin of the Atomic Scientists* 44: 36–42.

Olson, Mancur. 1965. *The Logic of Collective Action.* Cambridge, MA: Harvard University Press.

Olson, Mancur. 1982. *The Rise and Decline of Nations.* New Haven, CT: Yale University Press.

Powell, Robert. 1993. "Guns, Butter, and Anarchy." *American Political Science Review* 87: 115–132.

Reppy, Judith. 1985. "Military R & D and the Civilian Economy." *Bulletin of the Atomic Scientists* 41: 10–14.

Richardson, L.F. 1960. *Arms and Insecurity.* Pittsburgh: Boxwood Press.

Schumpeter, Joseph A. 1951. *Imperialism and Social Class.* Translated by Heinz Norden. New York: Augustus Kelley.

Simaan, M., and J.B. Cruz, Jr. 1975. "Formulation of Richardson's Model of Arms Race from a Differential Game Viewpoint." *Review of Economic Studies* 42: 67–77.

Smith, Ronald P. 1980. "Military Expenditure and Investment in OECD Countries, 1954–1973." *Journal of Comparative Economics* 4: 19–32.

Stockholm International Peace Research Institute. Published annually. *SIPRI Yearbook of World Armaments and Disarmament.* New York: Humanities Press.

Thompson, William R., and Gary Zuk. 1980. "World Power and the Strategic Trap of Territorial Commitments." *International Studies Quarterly* 30: 249–267.

Veblen, Thorstein. 1942. *Imperial Germany and the Industrial Revolution*. New York: Viking Press.

Waltz, Kenneth. 1979. *Theory of International Politics*. Reading, MA: Addison-Wesley.

World Bank. 1979 edition through 1994 edition. *World Development Report*. Oxford: Oxford University Press.

Wright, Quincy. 1965. *A Study of War*. Second Edition. Chicago: University of Chicago Press.

Table 5

European Market Economies: N=15

Dependent Variable
• Military spending as a percentage of GDP[17]

Independent Variable	*Coefficient*	*T-statistic*
• Income inequality[18]	17	3.5

R^2=0.49
Adj. R^2=0.45

European Market Economies: N=15

Dependent Variable
• Military spending as a percentage of GDP

Independent Variable	*Coefficient*	*T-statistic*
• Labor strength & unity[19]	–13	–0.8

R^2=0.04
Adj. R^2= –0.03

---

[17] Average, 1973–77. Author's calculations are based upon data from International Institute of Strategic Studies and the Stockholm Peace Research Institute.

[18] Gini index. For formula and sources of data, see chap. 1, note 51.

[19] Herfindahl index. For formula and sources of data, see chap. 1, note 52.

European Market Economies: N=15

Dependent Variable
- Military spending as a percentage of GDP

Independent Variables	*Coefficient*	*T-statistic*
• Income inequality	19	3.4
• Labor strength & unity	11	0.7

R^2=0.51
Adj. R^2=0.43

Central America/Caribbean: N=8

Dependent Variable
- Military spending as a percentage of GDP[20]

Independent Variable	*Coefficient*	*T-statistic*
• Income inequality	20	3.1

R^2=0.61
Adj. R^2=0.54

---

[20] Average, 1987–91.

Central America/Caribbean: N=8

Dependent Variable
- Military spending as a percentage of GDP

Independent Variable	*Coefficient*	*T-statistic*
• Labor strength & unity	–688	–2.3

R^2=0.47
Adj. R^2=0.38

Central America/Caribbean: N=8

Dependent Variable
- Military spending as a percentage of GDP

Independent Variables	*Coefficient*	*T-statistic*
• Income inequality	16	1.5
• Labor strength & unity	–239	–0.6

R^2=0.63
Adj. R^2=0.49

South America: N=7

Dependent Variable
- Military spending as a percentage of GDP[21]

Independent Variable	*Coefficient*	*T-statistic*
• Income inequality	−3	−0.4

R^2=0.03
Adj. R^2= −0.16

South America: N=7

Dependent Variable
- Military spending as a percentage of GDP

Independent Variable	*Coefficient*	*T-statistic*
• Labor strength & unity	−66	−3.2

R^2=0.67
Adj. R^2=0.60

---

[21] Average, 1988–92.

South America: N=7

Dependent Variable
- Military spending as a percentage of GDP

Independent Variables	*Coefficient*	*T-statistic*
• Income inequality	11	3.4
• Labor strength & unity	−102	−6.5

R^2=0.92
Adj. R^2=0.87

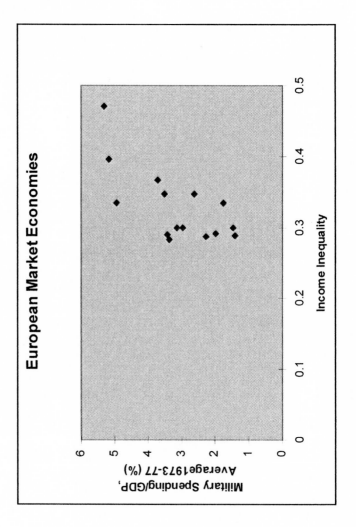

Figure 5.1

Figure 5.2

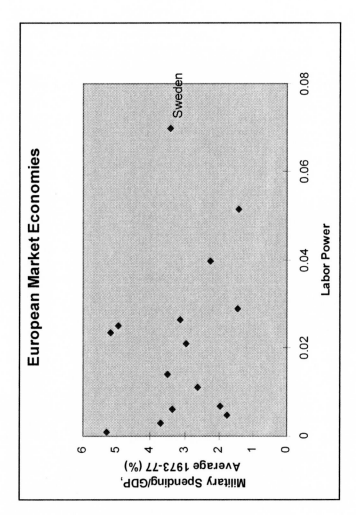

European Market Economies

Figure 5.3

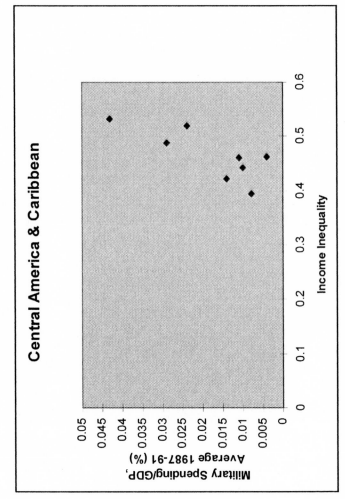

Central America & Caribbean

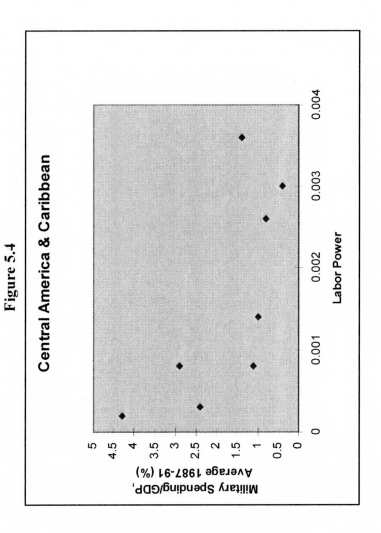

Figure 5.4

Central America & Caribbean

Figure 5.5

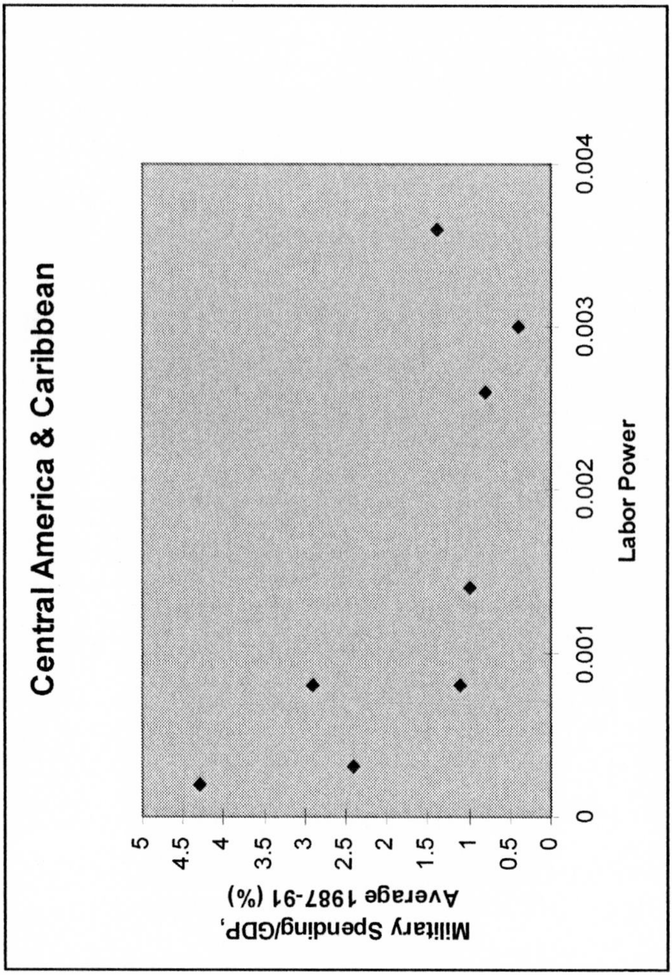

Central America & Caribbean

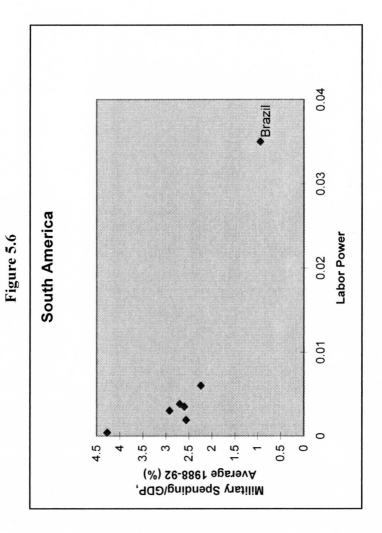

Figure 5.6

South America

6

Conclusions

Chapter 1 began with the question, "What's so great about democracy?" My answer is that democracy is desirable, not just because it is a fairer way of government than dictatorship, but also because it provides superior governance.

In fact, dispersed decision-making power yields better policies than centralized decision-making power. The more equally power is distributed in society, the more government policies tend to maximize aggregate social welfare.

This should come as no surprise to those readers who accept the superiority of democracy as an article of faith. After all, if you believe that people know what is best for them, then it stands to reason that the best policies are those that are shaped to the greatest degree by the people that they affect.

But not everyone believes that democracy is superior to dictatorship. It has become fashionable in many circles to extol the virtues of dictatorship. Many scholars and politicians argue that the remarkable economic success of countries such as Taiwan, South Korea, and Singapore is due to the enlightened governance of benevolent dictators. Democracy, so the argument goes, is too messy and inefficient to make a poor country rich. Only social harmony and sound economic policies enforced with adequate repression can force a country down the path of economic prosperity.

Such arguments should not be taken lightly. Many have argued that we are seeing the start of the reversal of the wave of democratization spawned by the demise of the Cold War. Newly democratic countries throughout the world have begun to reevaluate their chosen paths. Will their role model be Singapore or the United States? Only time will tell.

I hope that Part I of this book can serve as a counterweight to arguments in favor of dictatorship. I argue that the more equally power is distributed in society, the better. I have shown that a low degree of inequality in society tends to result in less severe political business cycles, higher economic growth rates, freer trade policies, and less wasteful military spending.

In addition, I have shown that domestic social factors, such as the distribution of income and the power of labor unions, can have a powerful impact upon those factors that make countries powerful internationally—economic growth rates and military spending. This, I hope, will counter the hypothesis amongst adherents of the realist theory of international relations that domestic factors are irrelevant to the international behavior of states.

Finally, I have tried to develop an analytical framework that transcends the boundaries of comparative politics and international relations. It is my hope that democratic efficiency analysis will help political scientists to look at some interesting problems from a new perspective, and perhaps serve as bridge between these two subdisciplines.

PART II

A Snapshot of Congress

Part II of this book describes the legislative process in the United States Congress. It is not meant to present a complete picture of that institution or the legislative process in all its complexity. Instead, it presents a "snapshot" of Congress at work. Like a snapshot, it displays a picture from a particular vantage point—in this case, the office of one member of the House of Representatives—and a particular point in time—in this case, a single week in spring 1999.

Part II of this book is entirely descriptive in nature. It does not evaluate any complex theories; nor does it engage in any statistical analysis. It merely describes what I observed during a week of unprecedented access to a portion of the legislative branch of the United States government.

In terms of classroom use, Part II is written in a style accessible to all students, regardless of background.

1

Those Who Work Behind the Scenes

Advising students is a significant portion of my job as a political science professor. Students often come to me to explore the possibility of pursuing a career working behind the scenes in Washington, D.C. This is something for which my otherwise excellent academic training did not prepare me; I had learned a lot about academic careers, but very little about careers on the applied side of politics. It was for this reason that I applied for a grant to look at politics from a career standpoint. The grant gave me the opportunity to spend a week "shadowing" Shelley Berkley, a freshman congresswoman from Nevada, to observe first-hand her interaction with staff and lobbyists. Now I can speak with a bit more authority when my students ask me to advise them about careers in Washington. Here is what I tell them.

Staff members do not just answer the phones for members of Congress. They play crucial and intensely powerful roles in the legislative process.

Each year, hundreds of bills—many of which are hundreds of pages long—cross the desks of members of Congress. There just is not time in their eighty-hour work-weeks for members of Congress to read all of these bills. Their staffs research the bills and advise them how to vote. The member, of course, makes the final decision, but it is rare that a member has the expertise to totally ignore the advice of his/her legislative staff.

Who are these staffers, and what sort of background do they have?

"Most people don't realize that the country is run by a bunch of twenty-five year olds," explains Vivian Huang, who works in the office of the Secretary of Health and Human Services. She is not exaggerating about their youth. Indeed, many key staff members are barely out of college.

Why are they so young? According to Richard Urey, Congresswoman Berkley's chief of staff, there are two reasons: a heavy workload and low pay. While most staff members do not have eighty-hour workweeks like members of Congress, neither do they work 9–5. Most staffers work late into the night on weekdays, and put in at least half a day on the weekends. Of course, long hours are also common for those holding powerful positions in the private sector. Congressional staffers are notable for the low salaries they receive for their hard work and long hours.

According to Urey, an entry-level staff position carries a starting salary of $18,000 to $20,000 per year, while most staffers with substantial legislative experience earn less than $30,000 per year.

Given the high workload and low salary, it is not surprising that most congressional staffers move on to another profession after a few years. Many go on to law school or other graduate studies. The fortunate few get promoted to jobs with more generous salaries, like committee staff members, legislative directors, or chiefs of staff. Some eventually cash in on their connections among the "power elite" and find highly-paid jobs as consultants or lobbyists. But the average congressional staffer starts young and moves on after just a few years.

The low salary and high workload must result, you might think, in a shortage of qualified applicants. Quite the contrary. There just seems to be something sexy about working amidst the corridors of power. (As Henry Kissinger once said, "Power is the ultimate aphrodisiac.") In fact, it is rare for a job opening to remain unfilled for more than a couple of days.

In order to get an entry-level job as a congressional staffer, you need a college degree and usually must have paid your dues by serving for several months as an unpaid intern on Capitol Hill.

Staff Assistant

The entry-level position is a staff assistant. This is usually the first person one comes into contact with, when arriving at the office of a member of Congress. S/he serves as a receptionist for guests, answers the phone, sorts the mail, books tours of the White House and other sites for visitors, and enters into a database the names of persons who contact the member's office.

Jane Bradshaw, Berkley's staff assistant, tells a fairly typical story of how she got her first job on Capitol Hill. She graduated from college in May 1998. After graduation, the Georgia native interned for one month with her local congressman. Next she interned for six months with the League of Conservation Voters. After the 1998 election, she began looking for a job on Capitol Hill, seeking, in particular, a pro-choice Democratic woman. This brought her to Berkley's office. She dropped off her resume on January 4, got interviewed by chief of staff Richard Urey and office administrator Marcie Evans, and started work on January 6, 1999.

Bradshaw enjoys her job, but finds it challenging at times. Sometimes she finds it difficult to be polite to rude constituents on the phone. But the most frustrating aspect of her job, she says, is when constituents call with genuine problems, and she knows that that Berkley's office is "not ... able to do anything to help them—outside of an act of Congress."

Bradshaw, a self-described liberal Democrat, hopes to work for Al Gore's presidential campaign, and then to get a job in a Gore White House. Afterwards, she plans to move back to Georgia and get involved in politics on the state level. Eventually, she hopes to follow in Berkley's footsteps and run for Congress.

Legislative Correspondent

After the staff assistant opens, sorts, and logs the letters, s/he passes them on to the legislative correspondent. Berkley receives about thirty letters on an average day, although she can receive many times that number when a particular issue in the news arouses the ire of her constituents. Cary Gibson, Berkley's legislative correspondent, reads and drafts responses to all of Berkley's letters from constituents. When she receives a large number of letters on the same issue, she drafts a form letter response. Berkley only reads those letters singled out by Gibson, such as a letter addressing an issue on which no one has previously written, or a letter containing an interesting suggestion. But Berkley reads all the responses which go out under her signature, and according to Gibson, Berkley often makes changes to them.

Legislative Assistants and Legislative Director

The legislative assistants, under the supervision of the legislative director, advise the member of Congress on issues of legislation. Each legislative assistant is responsible for a specific set of issues of public policy. In Berkley's office, there are two legislative assistants. Heather Cooper is responsible for foreign and defense issues (such as international relations, trade, human rights, veterans affairs, and military issues), plus energy and environmental issues. Maria Castillo handles most domestic issues, including transportation, health care, social security, and women's and children's issues.

A legislative assistant is responsible for researching each issue falling within his/her realm of responsibility, and formulating a position for the member of Congress. S/he writes speeches for the member, and briefs the member for public appearances. S/he also meets with lobbyists interested in particular pieces of legislation. The legislative assistant keeps track of legislation and advises the member on how to vote.

Cooper finds her job "very exciting, … always challenging, very fast-paced. You can't quite keep up with everything that's going on. You have to juggle issues and prioritize…. You find out at 2:00 p.m. that she [Berkley] needs a speech at 3:00 p.m. on a subject you don't know anything about."

Both Cooper and Castillo started off as interns in Washington. Each worked for at least one other member of

Congress before being hired by Berkley's office. Castillo explains that staff members commonly leave the office of one member of Congress after a year or two to accept a position of greater responsibility with another member. According to Cooper, the majority of the jobs on Capitol Hill are not advertised: "You've just got to stop by and drop your resume off. If the timing is right, you'll get a call if they need to replace someone right away."

Castillo and Cooper report to Mark Guiton, Berkley's legislative director. Guiton, a man with many years experience working behind the scenes on Capitol Hill, declined to be interviewed.

Press Secretary

The press secretary is responsible for maximizing the amount of positive coverage that the member receives in the media. According to Laura Chapin, Berkley's press secretary, she serves as a "conduit between the press in Las Vegas and what Shelley is doing here in Washington."

Chapin began her career in public relations for non-profit organizations. She got involved in several Democratic election campaigns in 1996, and then worked for two years for Sen. Barbara Mikulski (Maryland) before she was hired by Berkley.

Chapin received press training from EMILY's List, a political action committee that raises money for female Democratic candidates. This helped her to develop the contacts essential for doing a good job as press secretary. EMILY's List was an early contributor to Berkley's congressional campaign.

Office Administrator

The office administrator is the one staff member whose job has nothing to do with politics or constituents. Marcie Evans, Berkley's office administrator, instead is responsible for keeping the office running smoothly. She pays the bills, orders office supplies, arranges paychecks, schedules vacation time, interviews job applicants, supervises interns, and tries to ensure compliance with House rules and regulations.

Despite the nonpolitical nature of her job, Evans is highly partisan. When I asked her what was the most frustrating aspect of her job, she replied that it is that she "can't call the Republicans 'dogs.'"

Executive Assistant/Scheduler

The executive assistant/scheduler is responsible for ensuring that the member of Congress makes it through the day. Sloane Arnold, Berkley's executive assistant/scheduler has a wide range of duties. She puts together Berkley's daily schedule, and goes with her to many of the events on her schedule. She also screens the congresswoman's phone calls, and helps her with her personal correspondence.

Arnold is one of only two staff members with no prior experience in Washington. She met Berkley through her sorority at the University of Nevada, Las Vegas and helped with campaign fundraising for two years prior to Berkley's election to Congress.

Chief of Staff

The chief of staff supervises all staff, and is the primary advisor to the member of Congress on all issues. According to Richard Urey, Berkley's chief of staff, he sees himself as a strategist concerned with how Berkley can best use her time and resources to meet her political objectives.

Urey notes that a job in the political arena comes with pressures virtually unknown in the private sector: "Business is very competitive.... But it's not competitive in the sense that you get publicly attacked by people, or having the press looking ... for errors or foul-ups." Urey is responsible for avoiding errors and foul-ups.

Although Urey has never previously worked in Washington, he has an impressive resume. After moving to southern Nevada from California in the early 1980s, Urey worked in radio and TV news, before being hired as Nevada Governor Bob Miller's communications director in 1993. In 1998 he was hired as communications director in Berkley's campaign, and after she was elected, he assumed the position of chief of staff.

Lobbyist

Outside of Washington, lobbyist is a term of derision. On Capitol Hill, however, it is a highly sought-after title. Lobbyists, like staffers, work behind the scenes and wield a great deal of influence over public policy. But lobbyists work shorter hours, have greater job stability, and get paid a lot more than staffers. It is therefore not surprising that many staffers aspire to become lobbyists.

Jim DeChaine, like most lobbyists, started his career as a congressional staffer. During his twenty years as a staffer, he developed the contacts and expertise essential to becoming a successful lobbyist. The lobbyist from the Consumer Electronics Manufacturers Association is genial and easy to talk to—just the sort of qualities that help him to convince a member of Congress to listen to what he has to say.

Members of Congress may grab the headlines and cast the votes. But behind the scenes, armies of staffers and lobbyists shape our public policy.

Conclusion

When students ask me about a career behind the scenes in Washington, I tell them that they can expect an interesting and challenging job, but one in which they will work long hours for very low pay. If they stick it out, after a number of years they can expect to have a significant impact on shaping the debate on public policy. But most people don't stick it out, and instead move onto other endeavors after a few years.

After telling students all this, if they still are eager to give it a shot, I smile and give them my blessing. I then suggest that they seek an unpaid internship, one of the main prerequisites for getting a paid position.

2

A Week in the Life of
A Freshman Member of Congress

When I teach my students about the U.S. Congress, I find that they are familiar with two distinct perspectives on the institution. One—the more familiar of the two for most Americans—is the perspective presented by the media. Congress is an arena for speeches and debates, political maneuvering and soundbites. The other—the perspective presented in my students' textbooks—is an institution of democratic representation, an arena where interest groups battle for influence over public policy. Neither perspective, of course, presents the entire picture of what goes on in Congress. "What exactly does a member of Congress do on a day-to-day basis?" my students often ask me. I found that I did not know how to answer that question much better than they did.

Now I know the answer to this question, or, to be more precise, I know what a particular freshman member of

Congress did on a moment by moment basis during a random week in May 1999. I received a grant to spend a week "shadowing" Shelley Berkley, congresswoman from Nevada's 1st congressional district. Congresswoman Berkley told me to call her Shelley, and graciously allowed me to follow her nearly everywhere she went during that week.

This chapter will recount what the congresswoman did day-by-day, hour-by-hour, in an effort to provide an accurate representation of what the job of being a member of Congress actually entails.

Shelley has a grueling schedule. Her normal workday is at least fourteen hours long; her normal workweek six to seven days long. The public expects their elected representatives to be highly accessible and highly visible. Therefore, they must go out into the community and participate in activities ranging from barbecues to conventions to softball games and ice cream socials. According to her chief of staff, Richard Urey, Shelley receives an average of one hundred invitations to attend various events per month. According to her husband, Dr. Larry Lehrner, a nephrologist, Shelley is usually in Washington Mondays through Thursdays. On the weekend she's back in Las Vegas, but attends five to six events per day. This schedule must be hard on her family. "The main purpose of flying home on the weekends is to meet with her constituents," her husband explains. But he is very supportive of the work that she is doing.

What does Shelley do for fourteen hours per day in Washington? Let's take a look:

Sunday, May 23

I arrive in Washington. It is an unusual week for Shelley for two reasons. First of all, her husband Larry is there with her. Secondly, she has stayed in Washington over the weekend. Shelley and Larry are both in Washington to attend the America-Israel Public Affairs Committee (AIPAC) convention at the Washington Hilton. Several people told me that AIPAC is the most powerful lobby in Washington, after the American Association of Retired Persons. I believe them. More than half the members of Congress have come to their convention. AIPAC lobbies for strong ties between Israel and the United States.

Monday, May 24

I meet Shelley at the convention and interview her over a cup of coffee. She has been a member of AIPAC for many years, and is very supportive of the pro-Israel stance taken by the organization. This is the thirteenth convention that she has attended. I ask Shelley if her strong support of AIPAC is reciprocated by campaign contributions. She explains that AIPAC does not make campaign contributions, but through her long association with the organization, she has made many friends who contribute individually to her campaign.

At noon Shelley and I have lunch with participants in the convention, including the director of the Washington branch of the Anti-Defamation League.

Shelley explains that although she had wanted to be on the Foreign Affairs Committee, the Democratic leadership could not promise her a seat on the Middle East Subcommittee, and she had decided to serve on the Transportation Committee instead. Transportation is important for her home district—both in terms of expanding freeways in response to growth, and in terms of expanding the airport to facilitate the arrival of tourists.

1:15 p.m. Shelley and Larry depart to rest for a few hours.

6:15 p.m. Shelley returns to the convention for the banquet. It takes half an hour for the announcer to read off the list of hundreds of members of Congress and other distinguished guests. Shelley and I attend a reception after dinner. She makes her way through the crowd, chatting casually with old friends, campaign contributors, and other members of Congress.

11:00 p.m. Shelley and her husband depart. Shelley has a small apartment walking distance from her office.

Tuesday, May 25

8:30 a.m. Shelley listens to her phone messages. She puts one on speaker phone for me to hear: "Bill Clinton is a Nazi and a cocaine addict and is working for the Chinese!"

8:45 a.m. staff meeting. Topics discussed:
• a speech Shelley is scheduled to make later that day.

- Shelley supports moving the U.S. Embassy in Israel to Jerusalem (she will ask AIPAC to write a statement for her to read on the floor of House).
- Shelley will oppose peanut subsidies and sugar price supports (it will look good in the media if she takes a stand in support of responsible government fiscal policies).

9:00 a.m. Two men representing an optometrists organization lobby Shelley in her office. They urge her support for legislation requiring insurance companies to give patients access to optometrists. Shelley explains her strong support for a "patients' bill of rights."

9:25 a.m. Shelley calls someone back in her district to discuss a bill that will give Washington, D.C. students the right to pay resident tuition at all state colleges in the U.S.

A buzzer goes off and the clock on the wall in Shelley's office lights up. This usually indicates that she must go to the House floor to vote. It seems rather early, and Shelley checks. False alarm.

9:50 a.m. Shelley practices her speech.

10:00 a.m. Hearing at Committee on Resources. Topic: a proposal to ban aerial tours of the Grand Canyon. Supporters of the ban contend that the noise from aerial tours ruins the tranquility of the national park. Shelley makes a speech in opposition, citing potential harm to the tourist industry and Las Vegas economy. She also mentions that many elderly and disabled people are unable to see the Grand Canyon except by air.

10:40 a.m. Shelley meets with Richard Urey (her chief of staff) and Mark Guiton (legislative director) to discuss a gun control bill. They go through it point by point, discussing which provisions to support and which to oppose. Shelley decides to contact the police union, district attorney, and constable in Las Vegas to get their opinions.

11:20 a.m. Students from the AIPAC conference lobby Shelley. Shelley spends a great deal of time with them, giving them lots of encouragement. She speaks passionately in support of strong U.S. ties to Israel.

After lunch, Shelley goes to the House floor to vote. She stays there from 1:00 to 2:00 p.m. Only members of Congress are allowed on floor, so I sit in the Visitors' Gallery with Mark, her legislative director. No cameras or notebooks are allowed. Mark explains to me what is going on below on the House floor. We also discuss the degree to which members of Congress rely on their staff for information and advice when they must vote on legislation.

2:00 p.m. Shelley walks to the Democratic Congressional Campaign Committee building (DCCC) to meet Renee Aschoff (Shelley's campaign fund-raiser). Shelley explains that is illegal to conduct campaign-related business in her office, and therefore each party maintains a special building where members can go for fundraising purposes. Shelley describes it as one big room with lots of phones and no privacy. She and other Democratic congressmen sit there making phone calls requesting campaign contributions. Shelley apologizes that I cannot accompany her, because it would make donors and other members of Congress uncomfortable. I walk back to Shelley's office.

3:15 p.m. Just as Shelley returns to her office, her beeper goes off, signaling that she must vote. She runs back to the House, and I have to sit in the Visitors' Gallery again.

3:35 p.m. Shelley briefly leaves the floor to speak to Mark. Then Shelley goes back to the floor to vote again. Mark takes me to the Rayburn Room in the House. A few minutes later, Shelley meets me in the Rayburn Room. This is a good place for House members to meet with lobbyists on those occasions when the members cannot stray far from the floor because a vote is coming up. The room is quite posh, with big armchairs and oil paintings. Several members of Congress are holding meetings in various corners. Shelley meets there with a gentleman from Macy's representing the National Retail Association. He urges Shelley to support World Trade Organization membership for China, to oppose a national sales tax, and to oppose a patients bill of rights (which, he says, will likely cause insurance premiums to rise for employers). Shelley tells the lobbyist that she agrees with his position on the first two issues, but that she supports a patients bill of rights. The lobbyist does not seem disappointed. I guess two out of three is not bad.

4:15 p.m. Shelley returns to the floor to vote, and I return to the office with Renee and Sloane Arnold (Shelley's Executive Assistant). I interview several staff members.

5:00 p.m. I return to the Rayburn Room, where Shelley meets with lobbyists from the Service Employees International Union (SEIU). They urge support for the patients bill of rights. Shelley agrees to support it.

5:10 p.m. Shelley walks down the hall to Minority Leader Gephardt's office, in search of a quiet spot to make a phone call. She reviews her position on the Cox Committee report on Chinese nuclear espionage with Mark and Laura Chapin (her press secretary). Then Shelley calls a reporter in Las Vegas on her cell phone to discuss the Cox report.

5:30 p.m. Back to the Rayburn Room. A member of Mr. Gephardt's staff briefs Shelley on Medicare in preparation for her upcoming teleconference. They also discuss the possibility of co-sponsoring a bill on this subject.

5:50 p.m. Shelley returns to the floor to vote. I interview more of Shelley's staff members.

6:00 p.m. Shelley returns to her office. She calls Tod Story (her office manager in Las Vegas) to discuss her schedule for the days she will spend back in Las Vegas. While on the phone with Tod, Shelley's cell phone rings. The caller discusses concerns about red-lining of African Americans by banks. Shelley suggests holding a meeting between representatives of African Americans and banks. While talking on the phone, Shelley fixes her hair and makeup for her next engagement.

6:20 p.m. Shelley calls home and leaves a message, telling her kids that she is looking forward to seeing them over the weekend.

Shelley and Renee (her fundraiser) discuss whether Shelley should attend the American Gas Association meeting. Shelley asks how important this event is, whether they have made a campaign contribution, or whether they are expected to. Sloane says that they haven't yet, but they might. Shelley agrees to go.

6:30 p.m. Richard Urey (Chief of Staff) walks Shelley out to the street and confers privately with her on personnel matters. Then Shelley meets Larry for dinner.

7:45 p.m. I meet Shelley at the SEIU dinner. Shelley stands on stage with other congressmen, including Charles Rangel (New York), and she makes a speech.

8:30 p.m. Shelley has to leave for another vote on the House floor. After several votes, Shelley gets home by 9:30. It is an early night for her.

Wednesday, May 26

8:00 a.m. Breakfast meeting between lobbyists and Democratic members of the Transportation Committee. There is lots of schmoozing before the meeting begins. Topics of discussion at the meeting include bills to increase aviation funding (air traffic control, airport improvements, etc.), motor carrier safety, rail safety, and other issues. Shelley leaves shortly after the meeting begins.

8:35 a.m. We drive to Shelley's next breakfast meeting. Mark Guiton (Shelley's legislative director), Congressman Martin Frost (Texas), and Mark Angle of the Democratic Caucus crowd into the car with us. The meeting takes place at law offices of Meyers and Associates, in the Capitol Hill Office Building. We are greeted by members of Congressman Frost's staff. Mr. Frost has organized this meeting as a venue for Shelley to meet potential campaign contributors. The guests include representatives from SBC Communications, Lockheed Martin, the Distilled Spirits Association, Blue Cross Blue Shield, Union Pacific Railroad, and others. There is a lot of food, but most people are too busy schmoozing to eat.

The meeting begins, and Shelley makes a speech. She discusses the growth of her district, and the importance of the gaming and transportation industries. She mentions her committee assignments and the fact that she has the support of important interest groups in her district. Then she asks the lobbyists for their early support of her 2000 re-election campaign. Shelley explains that early money is essential for winning the election: she had declared her candidacy for the 1998 election the day after the 1996 election, and had begun raising money right away. She says she was advised by Rosa DeLauro (a veteran congresswoman from Connecticut): "If you think you're going to write the definitive piece of legislation on education this session—forget it! Go raise money!"

After the lobbyists leave, staff members of both congressmen huddle to discuss how they think things went.

10:00 a.m. Shelley returns to her office to prepare her remarks for her upcoming Medicare video conference. A couple of lobbyists from United Technologies show up and Shelley says hello to them before passing them off to Heather Cooper (legislative assistant).

10:40 a.m. Shelley meets with Sloane and Mark to work on Shelley's schedule. There are many more events to attend and people to meet than there is time in the day.

11:10 a.m. The meeting with the Aerial Tours lobbyist is canceled and Shelley continues her preparations for the video conference.

11:15 a.m. Maria Castillo (legislative assistant) meets with Shelley to help her prepare for the video conference.

11:30 a.m. Shelley meets privately with her former boss, who is now with Global Crossing, Ltd. I work on reviewing my notes.

Noon luncheon at Democratic Club with Congressman Ronnie Shows (Mississippi). On the way to the luncheon, Shelley runs into the Letter Carriers lobbyist in the hall and says hello.

After a quick drink, we sit down to lunch. There is a nice buffet. Shelley and I sit down at a table full of lobbyists.

One lobbyist, comments on the performance of Congressman Shows to one of the congressman's staff members: "He's doing a good job—keep him there."

"That's why *you're* here," replies the staff member.

"We just give the money," says the lobbyist playfully. "You [staff] do the work."

Term limits come up in the conversation. A consensus emerges that term limits prevent legislators from developing valuable experience and knowledge. One lobbyist sums it up: "If there were term limits, the staff would have all the power. Then they could, I suppose, put term limits on staff. Then we [lobbyists] would have all the power." He smiles mischievously. "Come to think of it, that's not a bad idea."

On the walk back to her office, Shelley runs into Congressman James Maloney (Connecticut), and says hello.

1:00 p.m. Shelley holds a video conference with Mr. Hatch, Medicare Administrator. A reporter and a photographer are present. The conference is held in the House TV studio. There is a fake backdrop of the Capitol and a bookcase containing law-related books (*Federal Reporter*, *US Treaties and Other International Agreements*, *Appellate Court Reports*, etc.). The studio is available to all House members. One usually must book the studio a week or two in advance. The Senate has its own studio. In addition, the

Democrats and the Republicans each have a separate studio in their respective party buildings.

Before the conference begins, some of Shelley's staff members discuss the prospects for local news coverage and "sound bites." Then Shelley and Hatch communicate via video with people back in Shelley's district.

2:40 p.m. Shelley's beeper goes off. Time to vote again. Shelley jumps on the Capitol subway. This is a private subway line connecting most of the House and Senate office buildings with the Capitol. I return to Shelley's office. After the vote, Shelley goes straight to the DCCC to make some more fundraising calls.

3:00 p.m. Since I can't attend fundraising calls, I visit the office of Senator Harry Reid (Nevada) and pick up a Senate gallery pass.

The Senate Chamber is smaller and more old-fashioned looking than the House chamber. Senators have small antique wooden desks. At the time of my visit, two senators are debating. No other senators are present. There are no microphones. Stenographers with machines suspended by straps walk from one senator to another, recording the debate.

5:20 p.m. Shelley and I take a cab to a nearby Mexican restaurant to attend a birthday party for Congresswoman Janice Schakowsky (Illinois). No one is there. We sit down at the bar and order some chips and salsa and iced tea.

I ask Shelley about fundraising. She tells me that she prefers to solicit contributions from people she knows. The Jewish community raised $1 million for her campaign before any strangers made any donations. She is very supportive of campaign finance reform, and finds it extremely frustrating that fundraising takes so much time away from her legislative duties. Shelley says that each political party has a publication listing groups that give campaign contributions. Members of Congress call up groups that are likely to support them. "I know that the Christian Coalition isn't going to give me any money," she explains as an example, and therefore she focuses her efforts on groups who are more likely to be supportive.

No one has shown up for the party, and Shelley calls to inquire on her cell phone. It turns out that the location of the party was changed, and the message never got to her. We walk back to her office.

5:40 p.m. Shelley meets with Dr. Ikram Khan, a friend of Shelley's who has been nominated for a federal appointment.

5:50 p.m. Shelley and Larry walk Dr. Khan to the Russell Senate Office Building to meet with some senators.

6:30 p.m. Shelley returns to her office. Shelley consults with Richard on an upcoming vote. She receives a "whip notice." This is instructions from the Democratic leadership on how to vote. The notice advises a "no" vote on the adjournment resolution, as a protest against Republican unwillingness to discuss campaign finance reform, gun control, and some other issues.

7:00 – 8:00 p.m. Shelley goes to vote, and I take the opportunity to get some dinner.

8:00 – 8:30 p.m. I watch the House floor from the visitors gallery. Then I call it a day.

Thursday, May 27

8:30–9:30 a.m. I have breakfast with Senator Harry Reid (Nevada), Assistant Minority Leader. On Thursday mornings he hosts a continental breakfast in his office for constituents who are in Washington. Half a dozen people attend. A photographer takes a picture of each guest with the senator.

10:00 a.m. I meet Shelley in room 2167, Rayburn Building. The Transportation Committee engages in a bill "markup" session. Shelley whispers back and forth with the congressman sitting next to her, while the committee chair and the ranking minority member of the committee each make speeches praising the bill.

11:10 a.m. Shelley returns to her office. She discusses with Mark whether to endorse Bill Bradley or Al Gore for President. Shelley says she doesn't know Bradley but likes Gore. Mark suggests that Bradley is more liberal than Gore. Shelley replies that Gore opposes building a nuclear waste dump in Nevada, and that he is pro-gaming. She says she will endorse Gore.

11:15 a.m. Shelley reviews letters, newspaper clippings, memos, and other documents compiled by her staff.

I speak to Mark. He explains that the House leadership decides how many seats on each committee are allocated to each party. Theoretically, the House Republican leadership could give the Republicans all the seats and the Democrats none. But if they did this the Democrats would refuse to cooperate with them (for example, they might vote no on everything as a protest). In practice, the majority party gets a higher proportion of seats on each committee than the actual partisan ratio in the House, but the advantage is not unreasonably large. Once each party finds out how many seats they are allocated for each committee, the party leadership decides who sits on each committee. Members with higher seniority are more likely to get their first choices.

11:35 a.m. Democratic Caucus meeting. Lots of reporters, photographers, and cameramen are present. Vice President Al Gore and Minority Leader Richard Gephardt make speeches on the juvenile justice bill. Democratic members of Congress—including Shelley—surround them on the stage.

12:15 p.m. Meeting ends. Members of Congress file out into the hall and line up for satellite feeds. Each member is asked to stand in front of a camera and state his/her name and district. Then s/he makes a short statement about the bill.

Laura tells me that she will notify Las Vegas TV stations that Shelley's remarks are available for broadcast.

12:30 p.m. Shelley and I take a cab to Senate Park for a rally by Jewish War Veterans. The vets' leader makes a speech voicing anger at cuts in veterans' benefits. Shelley makes a speech in support of greater funding for veterans.

After she finishes her speech, Associate Press reporter Larry Arnold asks Shelley what she thinks of federal regulation of casinos. Shelley tells him that she opposes it.

1:20 p.m. We walk back to Shelley's office.

1:45 p.m. Shelley and I have lunch in the cafeteria in the Longworth Building, where her office is located. Shelley tells me that she is frustrated that the Republicans won't let the House pass laws on campaign finance reform and other issues important to her.

I ask Shelley about the factors influencing the way she votes. She explains that sometimes she will vote based on her personal convictions, and sometimes she will let her vote be swayed by public opinion. She explains that she is pro-choice and "no poll in the world is going to change my opinion." In contrast, she explains that she is a member of the ACLU, and "if I'd been told a year ago that I'd be supporting a flag burning amendment, I wouldn't have believed it. But veterans are so supportive of this. I've seen battle-hardened veterans with tears in their eyes when they talk about the flag. It's really important to them." Shelley had recently voted in favor of a constitutional amendment banning flag burning.

2:15 p.m. Shelley meets with Laura and Mark to discuss various issues, including the proposed tax on employee meals. Then Shelley calls a reporter back in Las Vegas to let him know her schedule for the upcoming weekend—which she will be spending back in Las Vegas. Shelley indicates that she will be meeting with representatives of small businesses to discuss government assistance with their Y2K preparations.

Mark mentions that the Democrats are moving away from using the term "sampling" because it isn't polling well. The Democrats have favored using statistical sampling techniques in the census because poor people and minorities disproportionately tend to get left out of the count. Republicans oppose this, believing that the census should only count people who are contacted directly by census takers. This is an important issue, because billions of federal government dollars—as well as seats in the House—are allocated to the states based on population.

2:30 p.m. Shelley meets with Cary Gibson (legislative correspondent) to go over letters that Cary has drafted in response to letters that Shelley had received from her constituents.

2:50 p.m. Shelley meets with Richard. Shelley calls the chair of the Nevada Democratic Party to discuss a bill that would move the primary election to an earlier date. Democrats oppose this, feeling that the change of date would benefit Republicans. After the call, Shelley meets privately with Richard. I go out to the reception area.

Lobbyists from the Consumer Electronics Manufacturers Association are waiting to meet with Shelley. I chat with them about their careers as lobbyists.

4:00 p.m. The lobbyists and I are invited into Shelley's office. The meeting is very chatty. It is an opportunity for the lobbyists and the congresswoman to get to know one another. Shelley discusses her ties to AIPAC, as well as casino owner Sheldon Adelson's attempts to defeat her in the election by bankrolling her opponent. The lobbyists invite Shelley to an electronics trade show scheduled to occur in Las Vegas during the following January.

Shelley mentions that she had spent $1.4 million on her previous campaign and that she was left with a $47,000 debt. She notes that House Democratic leader Dick Gephardt had promised her a seat on the Ways and Means Committee if the Democrats receive a majority in the next election. House members with seats on the Ways and Means Committee are able to raise lots of campaign funds, because Ways and Means is the most powerful committee in the House.

4:20 p.m. Shelley discusses flight arrangements with Sloane Arnold (her executive assistant). She tells Sloane to send Renee (her fundraiser) a cake for her birthday.

4:25 p.m. Private meeting with Mark and Heather. I chat with Larry about what it is like being married to a congresswoman.

5:00 p.m. The House has adjourned for the holiday weekend. I help Shelley and Larry carry their luggage down to the taxi. They head for the airport to fly home for the weekend.

Friday, May 28

10 a.m. to 3 p.m. I conduct more interviews with Shelley's staff, and take some video footage of the Capitol and the Longworth Building.

3

The Paradox of Power

The work of Congress is hidden behind several familiar façades. One is the façade of a grand debating chamber whose inhabitants are steeped in the philosophies of Locke and Rousseau, as interpreted by the esteemed founders of the Republic. Another façade is constructed of the images and soundbites that the media project into American households. I often had wondered what, if anything, lies behind these façades.

In May 1999, I had a unique opportunity to take a peek. I received a grant to spend a week "shadowing" Congresswoman Shelley Berkley, a first-term Democratic congresswoman from Nevada's 1st congressional district. I followed the congresswoman through her day-to-day activities for a whole week, attending meetings with staff members and lobbyists, committee meetings, press conferences, rallies, and even conversations with family and friends. This experience gave me a fuller understanding of the institution we call Congress, as seen from the perspective of those who work there. This chapter will share my impressions of some of the shortcomings of our system of government that came to light during this experience.

There are two sides to Congress: one public, one private. The public side is what you see on TV. The rule of thumb in Washington is that anything done in front of a TV camera has absolutely nothing to do with public policy and absolutely everything to do with public relations. The speeches from the House floor that you watch? The congressmen and senators are making speeches to an empty room. What about the debates? No one is present besides the two people debating, plus a few stenographers. Remarks about some current topic in the news? Written by staffers or lobbyists, carefully scripted to be broken up into 10-second soundbites that convey no relevant information, but get the politician's face on the evening news.

In fact, it would not be an exaggeration to say that the House and Senate chambers are anachronisms maintained mostly for tourists. Gone is the era when members of Congress spent their days hurling rhetorical barbs at each other across the floor. In fact, congressmen rarely set foot on the floor except to vote or to make speeches to hundreds of empty seats in the hopes that their remarks will end up on TV.

Members of Congress consider going to the floor a nuisance that takes time away from the more important aspects of their jobs. They wear beepers that alert them when it is time to vote. As soon as the votes are finished, they rush back to whatever they were doing. For efficiency sake, it would make a lot more sense for them to call in their votes over their cell phones. But, of course, then the tourists and TV viewers would have nothing to watch.

If they don't spend much time debating bills, what exactly do members of Congress do during their eighty-hour workweeks? The vast majority of their time is spent trying to get re-elected.

Welcome to the era of the continuous campaign. Virtually everything that members of Congress do follows a careful analysis of its likely impact on voters and campaign contributors.

Don't get me wrong—this is not an indictment of our members of Congress. To my great astonishment, given the brutal and bizarre vetting process to which the news media subject candidates, Congress contains quite a number of noble individuals. But like any quarry, the survival instincts of a politician must take precedence over the nobler instincts. Otherwise, the politician is a dead duck.

Members of Congress spend most of their time talking to people. They are troubleshooters first, legislators second. Their primary job is to listen to your problems, appear sympathetic, and take some action—however hopeless the situation may be—to help you. They meet with veterans concerned about cuts in veterans benefits. They meet with senior citizens concerned about the future of Medicare and Social Security. They meet with parents concerned about funding levels in public schools. The list goes on and on. Members of Congress run themselves ragged lending a sympathetic ear to groups of constituents who are concerned about all sorts of problems. There is absolutely nothing ignoble about this. In fact, I think that it is a good thing that our legislators listen to the public. The downside, however, is that very little time is left for discussing how to solve our nation's problems. The big picture gets lost in the details.

Of course, congressmen don't spend all their time meeting with people like you and me. Much of the time, they meet with people who cannot cast a single vote for them, but whose support is essential to their hopes of reelection: campaign contributors.

In 1996, persons winning election to the House of Representatives spent an average of $647,000 on their campaigns.[1] In the 2000 election, winners spent more than $840,000 each, on average. For the Senate, comparable figures are $4.7 million and $7.5 million. This is an awful lot of money, especially when you consider that no individual can contribute more than $2,000 to any given candidate, and no political action committee more than $5,000. Members of Congress seeking reelection therefore find it necessary to attend an endless series of breakfasts, lunches, and dinners, at which the member must market him/herself like a brand of toothpaste or laundry detergent. In addition, members of Congress must spend every spare moment on the phone begging for money from strangers on a list of prospective contributors.

Why on earth would anyone want a job like this? I kept asking myself this question as I observed the workings of Congress. The best answer I can come up with is that you have got to love the spotlight and be irrationally optimistic about your chances of having a positive impact upon the body politic.

---

[1] Center for Responsive Politics, www.opensecrets.org.

If you ask a member of Congress like Shelley Berkley why she would volunteer for an eighty-hour-a-week job in which people are constantly attacking her personal integrity and character, she invariably replies that she hopes to make a difference. If you press hard enough, you may get the congresswoman to admit that her largest source of frustration is that all the media appearances and meetings with constituents and lobbyists leave little time to tackle the problems of our country. But then she will sigh, and recite the mantra, "If I can just get past the next election, I know that things will be different. Then I'll have time to improve the lives of millions of people by writing the definitive piece of legislation fundamentally reforming...."

Of course, once this election is past, the next one looms. There never seems to be enough time. Meanwhile, the rest of us muddle through without those fundamental reforms.

If our elected officials are so busy with the constant campaign, how do laws get passed? Are they voting on bills that they never read?

Yes. But I hasten to add that things are not quite as bad as they seem. Members of Congress get substantial advice on how to vote from lots of very knowledgeable people—some of whom have even taken the time to read the bill in question.

A congressman's legislative staff advises him/her on how to vote. But even they often do not have the time to read through all of the hundreds of bills—many of which are hundreds of pages long—for which they are responsible. From whom do they get their information? Committee staff and lobbyists.

Each bill under consideration goes through at least one committee. The committees are served by staffers whose job it is to scrutinize the bills that come under their jurisdiction. If anyone at all reads the bills, they do. They give advice to members of Congress and their legislative staffs on the pros and cons of various bills.

Lobbyists don't always read the bills themselves. But they represent groups whose lawyers have scrutinized carefully bills for their likely impact on the group's interests. Lobbyists are therefore eager to advise members of Congress and their legislative staffs on the pros and cons of particular bills: "This provision will cost my industry $242 million dollars and 8,000 voters will lose their jobs as a result."

Couldn't the committee staff members and lobbyists give false and misleading information, causing a member of Congress to vote for something that s/he would otherwise disagree with? In theory, yes. In practice, it rarely happens.

Think about it. Access and influence are the hot commodities in Washington. Members of Congress rely on you for information. If you mislead them, they will never listen to you again. No more access, no more influence. Most likely, no more career for you. Yes, you can try to spin the information to your own benefit. But you can't lie or mislead—or at least, not more than once.

Members of Congress don't always wait for interested parties to come to them with advice. Sometimes they seek them out. Congresswoman Berkley, for example, decided to solicit the views of the police union, district attorney, and constable back in Las Vegas on a complicated piece of crime legislation.

You are probably wondering, if the members of Congress are too busy to read the bills they are voting on, how on earth do they find the time to write the bills in the first place. Once again, they don't. Although members of Congress are listed as the authors of particular bills, staff members and lobbyists tend to be the ghost writers. In fact, it is not unheard of for a lobbyist to present a complete bill to a staffer who, with the member's approval, introduces it for consideration in Congress.

This leads to the key question about Congress: who knows the big picture? One law can affect millions of individuals and thousands of businesses, and interact in unexpected ways with other laws and regulations. The answer: *no one* knows the big picture.

The United States Congress is not the elegant debating chamber shown to the tourists. It is a byzantine organization in which a multiplicity of interest groups vie for the ears of bright kids just out of college, who in turn advise your elected representatives on how to vote. The job of your member of Congress is part public relations and part fundraiser, with rather little time left to tackle the public policy issues s/he holds so dear. This is a source of great frustration for members of Congress.

It is easy to attack Congress, and easy to attack the politicians that make it up. Certainly there are some bad apples. But I was struck by the commitment to the public service displayed by most of the people I met in Washington. It is not really their fault that the system is set up the way it is. They just do their best with a bad system.

Why can't they do better? Let's say that after you got elected to the House of Representatives for the first time, you decided that you would not run for a second term. You would eschew the media, lobbyists, and campaign contributors, and spend all your time writing and scrutinizing legislation. That means that you would have a two-year time limit to make your mark on public policy. Most laws introduced in Congress never even come to a vote (they die in committee), so chances are slim that you will get any fundamental reforms passed. Even worse, your focus on crafting exquisite legislation, rather than on coalition building and garnering public support through the media, will likely leave you devoid of the support you need to get things passed. You most likely will accomplish nothing at all.

That is why I say that members of Congress are irrationally optimistic. They desperately want to pass fundamental reforms, but know that if they focus their energies on this task, they will get nowhere. So they focus their energies on public relations and fundraising, and keep repeating the mantra, "If I can just get past the next election, I know that things will be different...."

About the Author

Lee Ryan Miller earned a Ph.D. in political science from the University of California, Los Angeles (UCLA). He also is the author of a book on international relations theory, *Confessions of a Recovering Realist: Toward a Neo-Liberal Theory of International Relations.* In addition, he is the author of *Teaching Amidst the Neon Palm Trees*, a memoir of his experiences teaching at a college in Las Vegas. He currently is a Lecturer in political science at California State University, Stanislaus. You may visit his website at www.LeeRyanMiller.com

Printed in the United States
28635LVS00001B/31-45